A Guide to
Peril Strait and Wrangell Narrows, Alaska

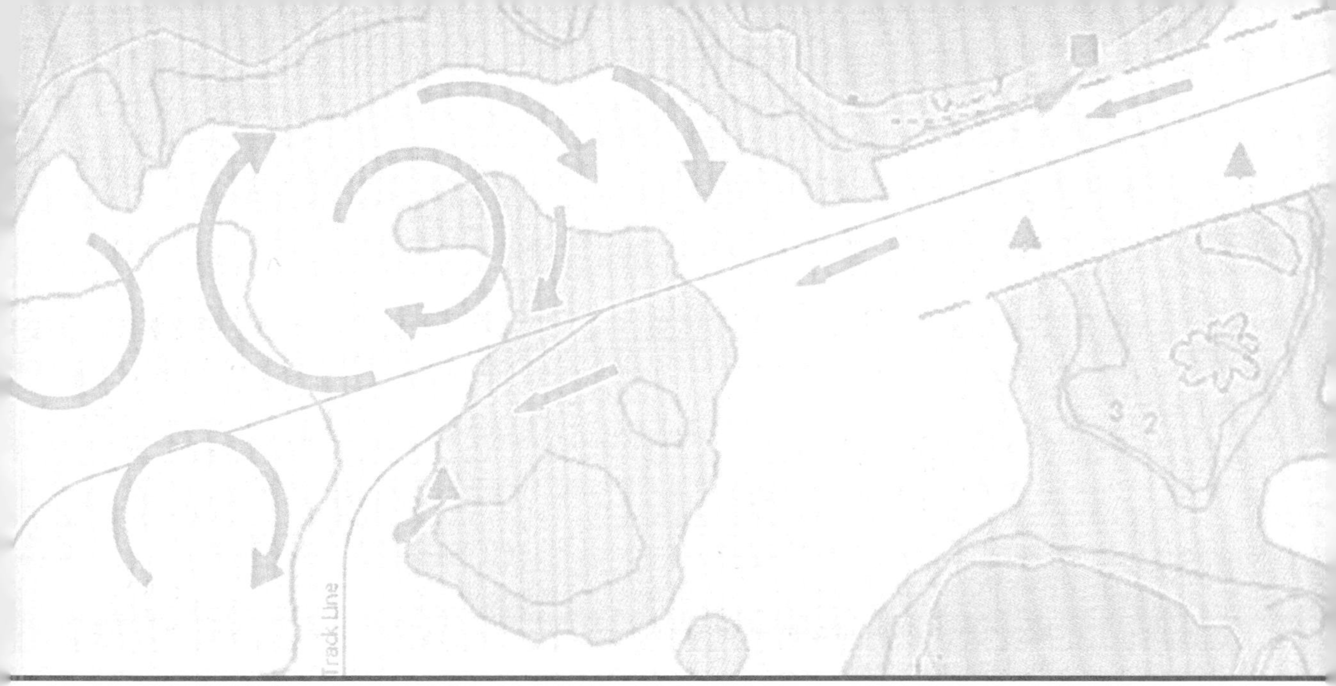

A GUIDE TO PERIL STRAIT AND WRANGELL NARROWS, ALASKA

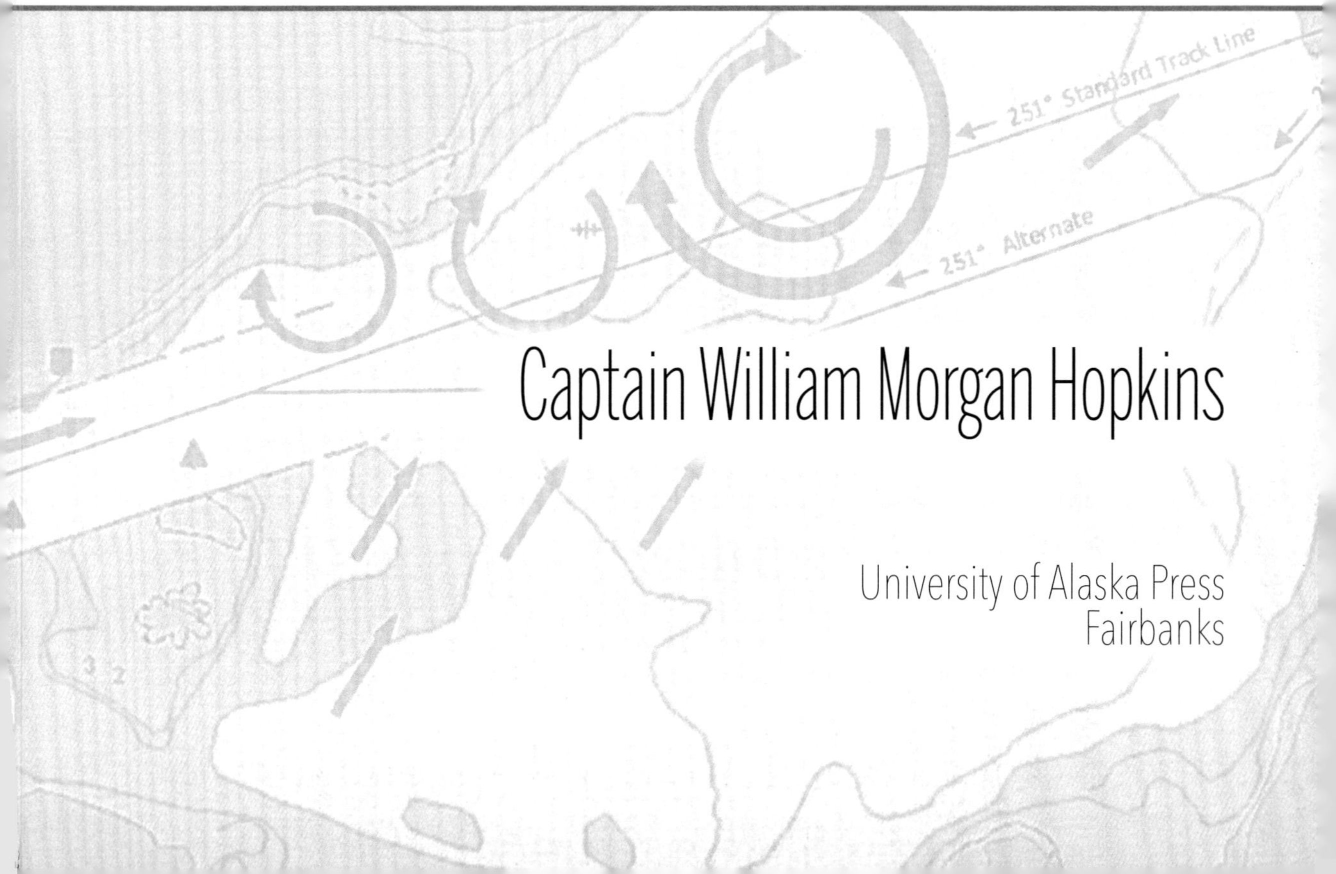

Captain William Morgan Hopkins

University of Alaska Press
Fairbanks

Revised and updated on August 12, 2015, May 15, 2019

Published by
University of Alaska Press
P.O. Box 756240
Fairbanks, AK 99775-6240

Cover and interior design by Paula Elmes.

Library of Congress Cataloging-in-Publication Data
LCCN 2019949461

PRINTED IN CANADA

Dedicated to the officers and sailors of the
Alaska Marine Highway System,
past and present

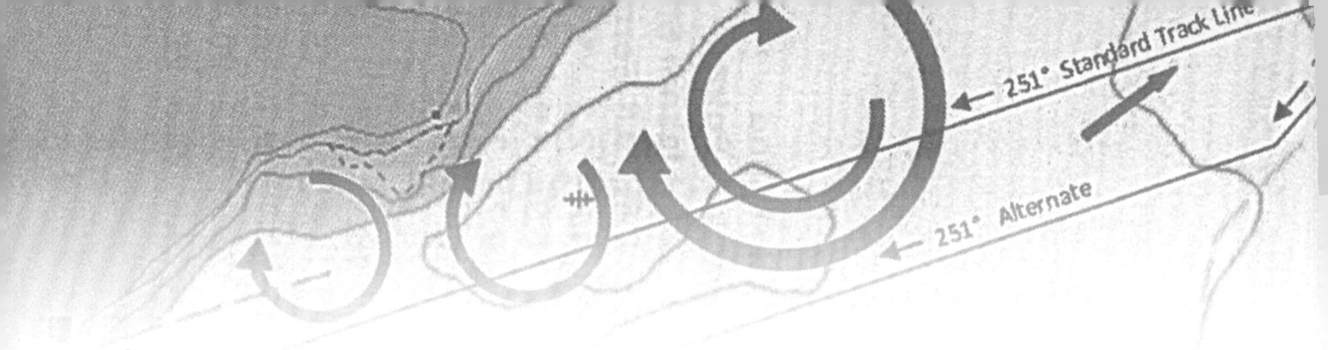

Contents

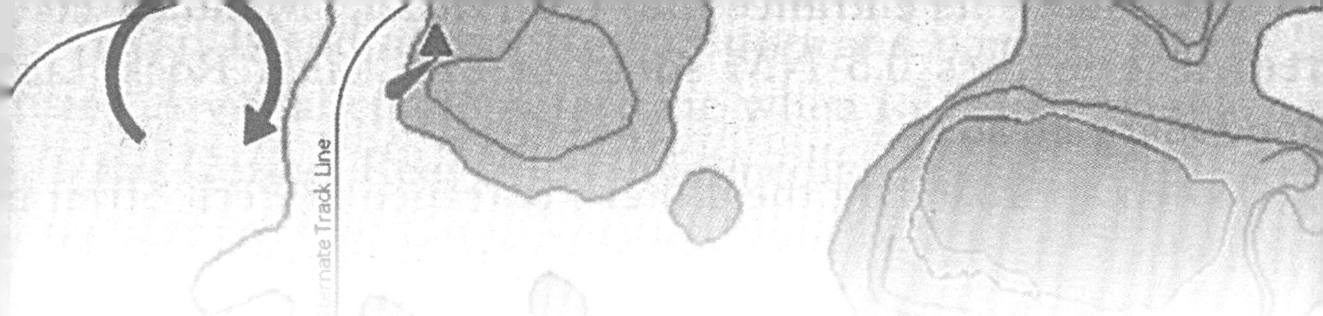
Alternate Track Line

Terminology

The courses are given in degrees true, reading clockwise from 000° at north to 359°. For example, when a course is given as 050°, this means the true course to be made good.

Distances are in nautical miles (NM).

Multiply nautical miles by 1.15 to obtain approximate statute miles. A nautical mile is 6076.1 feet and equal to one minute of latitude.

Depths are in fathoms and feet below mean lower low water.

Currents are expressed in knots (nautical miles per hour).

The directions of winds are the points from which the wind blows. The directions of currents are the points toward which they flow.

EBL refers to electronic bearing line, and VRM indicates variable range marker with regard to radar usage.

Stemming means going against the current, as contrasted with going with the current.

Conning is to direct the helmsman as to the movements of the helm for steering.

Holdover refers to the depth of water above the zero-foot tide (chart datum) line or the depths published on the chart.

Abeam means at a right angle to the line of the keel of a vessel.

One shot of anchor chain equals 90 feet.

Peril Strait

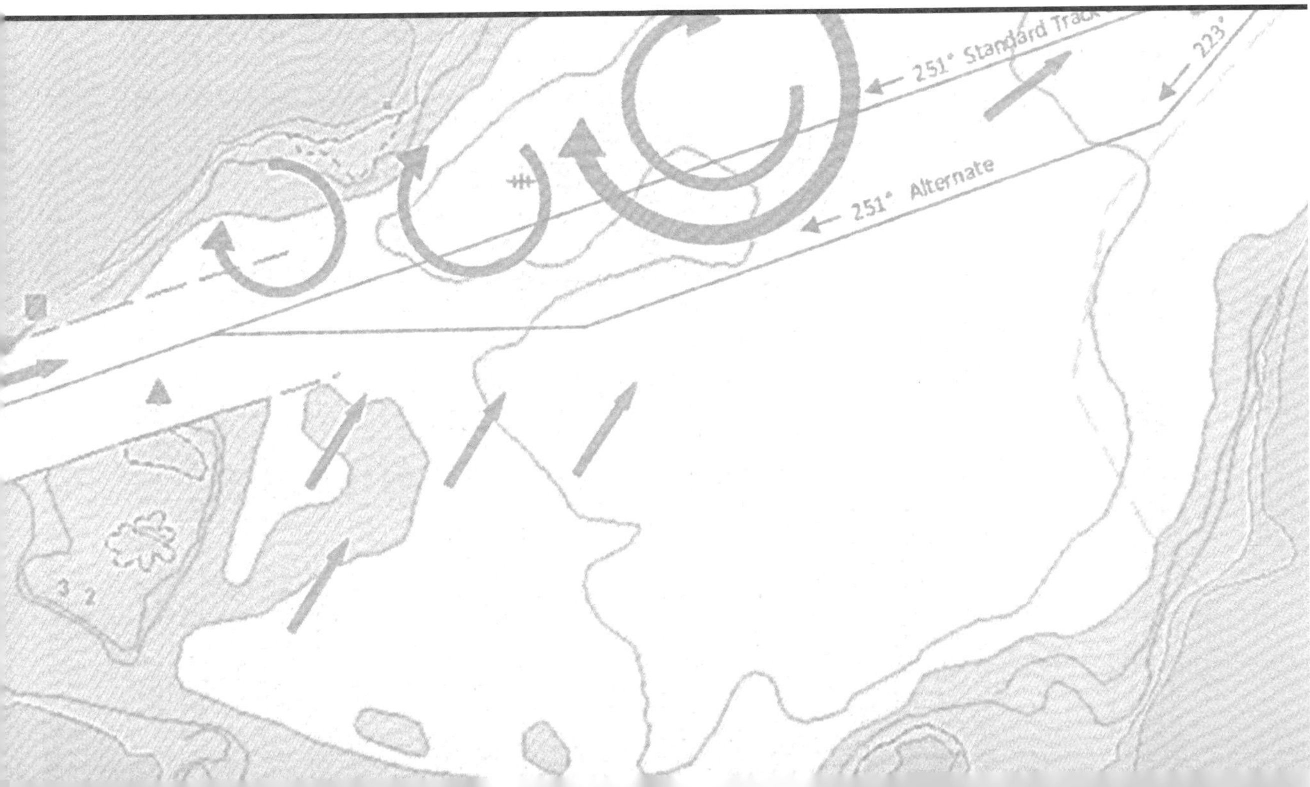

Introduction to Peril Strait

Peril Strait in Southeastern Alaska bisects Chichagof Island and Baranof Island from east to west. One of Alaska's more historic waterways, Peril Strait provides an inside route to the city of Sitka from Chatham Strait on the Inside Passage.

The easternmost reaches of Peril Strait are wide and deep, trending southeast and eastward to their junction with Chatham Strait. The western two-thirds, however, are narrow and hazardous, with strong currents that necessitate numerous course changes.

The main body of Peril Strait extends from Morris Reef in the east to Kakul Point in the west. When navigators refer to Peril Strait, they also include Neva Strait and Olga Strait. Technically, this is incorrect. Peril Strait terminates at Kakul Point, where the strait exits into Salisbury Sound through Kakul Narrows.

Neva and Olga Straits continue the inside route into Sitka. A short distance beyond Kakul Point is the head of Salisbury Sound, located at Scraggy Island. From Scraggy Island, Neva Strait begins wending its way to Whitestone Narrows and Neva Point, separating Baranof Island from Partofshikof Island.

Across from and south of Neva Point is Olga Point and the beginning of Olga Strait, which separates Halleck Island and Baranof Island from Krestof Island and the Siginaka Islands of Sitka Sound. Olga Strait takes the traveler the final distance to Sitka.

Neva and Olga Straits connect Sitka Sound with Salisbury Sound, while Peril Strait connects Salisbury Sound (in the Gulf of Alaska) with Chatham Strait (in the Inside Passage). There are dangerous shoals, rocks, reefs, and strong tidal currents to consider when navigating these waterways. Inserted within these straits are Sergius Narrows in Peril Strait and Whitestone Narrows at the southern end of Neva Strait.

These are intricate and beautifully scenic waterways. Peril Strait retains much of its wild character, despite a long history of cannery operations, mining, and logging operations along its shores. Careful observers may view Alaska brown bears and Sitka black-tailed deer along the shorelines or even swimming across the channels. In season, feeding humpback whales may also be seen.

These passages form a natural marine highway of commerce, carrying a significant amount of vessel traffic. Tugboats towing barges, ferries of the Alaska Marine Highway System, Coast Guard buoy tenders and patrol boats, charter vessels, pleasure craft, and commercial fishing vessels of all varieties ply these waters. In the past, vessels towing log rafts to Sitka frequently used the waterway.

This section describes piloting these connecting saltwater passages. It is a means of preserving the piloting methods taught by the older captains and pilots of the Alaska Marine Highway System for the safe navigation of Peril Strait. Their knowledge was hard-won, coming from long experience. The information herein serves as an aid to new generations of navigators so that they may learn in detail the intricacies of these demanding channels. It is hoped that this information is helpful and practical for navigators who travel through these waters. Although the methods described in this guide may not fully apply to smaller vessels, they should be helpful nonetheless.

The information contained in this guide represents years of accumulated knowledge by masters and pilots of the Alaska Marine Highway System. It is written for general interest only and is not intended to be the complete, definitive, and specific rule or method for navigation of these waterways. It does not supersede or contradict information found within the *Coast Pilot,* applicable charts, or any official government publications and documents that pertain to the navigation of this area.

It is the responsibility of each individual vessel master to exercise proper judgment with regard to due diligence and to the practice of good seamanship. These duties appropriately rest upon each vessel master.

Navigating Peril Strait

Native Tlingit people have used Peril Strait, Neva Strait, and Olga Strait for thousands of years. The cultural history dates back 9,000 years, and most likely even farther. In comparison, Russian, Spanish, French, and English explorers came only recently. These explorers, however, began to describe Alaska's coast and waterways in writing and render them onto nautical charts.

Alaska became a Russian territory in the eighteenth century, falling under the purview of the Russian American Company and its powerful Russian managers and traders. The Russian American Company eventually headquartered in Sitka, making the town its principal establishment and the Russian capital of Alaska.

Company employees, hunters, sailors, and pilots used these waterways to their advantage. They learned them well, leaving behind many of the local place names still found in use today.

Peril Strait was officially named in 1833 by the Russians to commemorate the largest paralytic shellfish poisoning occurrence in Alaska's history. In 1799, a large party of Aleut hunters led by Alexander Baranov had stopped near Poison Cove to harvest mussels. The exact site remains unknown. Within several hours, however, 150 Aleut hunters were said to have perished. Nearby Povorotni Island (Russian for *turnabout*), Pogibshi Point (*perilous*), and Deadman's Reach further allude to this tragic event.

In the fall of 1805, as Lewis and Clark were making their epic journey down the Columbia River to the Pacific Ocean:

> two adventuresome fellows made a canoe trip from New Archangel, as Sitka was then known, to the eastern end of Peril Strait. They were Captain John D'Wolf, an American fur trader who had just sold his ship to the Russians, and George Langendorf. Both were working in the service of the Russian American Company.
>
> Both men later wrote about their journey. They knew that the Russians had gone through Peril Strait, including Sergius Narrows, with ships up to 150 tons. D'Wolf said that he had never anywhere seen such a rush of water and he considered the Russians extremely adventurous to put themselves and a ship in such a hazardous place.[1]

When the Americans purchased Alaska from the Russians in 1867, they knew very little about their newly acquired territory. It is interesting to read from *Coast Pilot of Alaska, First Part, From Southern Boundary to Cook's Inlet,* written by George Davidson in 1869, to see how sparse the knowledge of this area was at the time. Much of the information contained in this classic volume comes from Native and Russian sources (Tebenkof) and from those of the great explorers—La Pérouse, Cook, Portlock, and Vancouver. It shows clearly that the Americans had much to learn about the coast of Alaska. With Davidson began the long process of geographical reconnaissance, surveying, and the gaining of hard-won knowledge to be placed in future *Coast Pilot*s and on American nautical charts that continues to this day.

Davidson noted that "a good passage exists . . . and continues through Peril Strait to Chatham Strait. The Coast Survey has made several preliminary examinations through these waters, and changed materially their shape on the English chart. But they should not be run without a pilot of good local knowledge."

1 Robert N. DeArmond, "Peril Strait, Part 9, Around & About Alaska, Notes and Comments," *Sitka Sentinel,* December 24, 1998.

Davidson continues:

> Neva Passage, leading from the north entrance of Olga Strait to Peril Strait, is quite narrow [Whitestone Narrows], and has numerous sunken rocks along its shores. The Coast Survey made a preliminary examination of it, which indicated plenty of water, but made the passage narrower than laid down on the charts. With a thorough survey of this strait and Salisbury Sound, with its bold approaches, another entrance is afforded to Sitka Sound to vessels driven north of Cape Edgecumbe by heavy southeasters or by the currents in light airs.[2]

Both Olga and Neva Straits are named for Russian ships. According to Klebnikof, an early biographer of Alexander Baranov, Baranov rounded Cape Edgecumbe by way of a hitherto-unknown strait on his way to establish a settlement at Sitka. This passage was christened after S/V *Olga,* a small vessel with one mast and one deck, built in Resurrection Bay (Seward), Alaska, in 1795.[3]

The *Neva,* on the other hand, was a full-rigged ship, purchased in England by the Russian American Company. It sailed from the Baltic Sea around Cape Horn to Alaska in 1803, a route commonly used by the Russians to travel to their Alaska possession. The *Neva* participated in the fight against the Tlingit over the establishment of a permanent Russian settlement at Sitka.

After the fighting, the *Neva* continued her voyage around the world, eventually returning to the Baltic. This stout vessel made a second voyage to the Russian colony of Alaska and remained in

---

2 George Davidson, *Coast Pilot of Alaska: First Part, From Southern Boundary to Cook's Inlet* (Washington: Government Printing Office, 1869), 121–22.

3 Patricia Roppel, unpublished and undated history notes on Peril Strait, Neva and Olga Straits, Wrangell, Alaska, c. 1990.

the Pacific in the service of the Russian American Company until wrecking on Kruzof Island near Sitka in January 1813.[4]

Davidson cautioned of Peril Strait:

> This strait, leading from the northeast part of Salisbury Strait to Chatham Strait, has a tortuous channel, with a general north-northeast direction for ten miles, with an average width of three-quarters of a mile.
>
> It is used by the Russian vessels. The navigation of this strait, until better known, should be made under the direction of a pilot, and at or near slack-water low tide, as there are several narrow places where the currents and counter-currents are very strong and dangerous to a side-wheel steamer.[5]

It is not hard to imagine the difficulties of navigating Peril Strait with a large sailing ship. *Pacific Coast Pilot—Alaska, Part 1, 1883* warns of the hazards of Peril Strait: "strong and turbulent tidal currents . . . rendered dangerous and difficult of navigation even for steam-vessels, and should on no account be attempted without a pilot or by any sailing vessel of considerable size."[6]

However, with steamship navigation on the rise, Peril Strait became a more practical alternative for protecting vessels on inside waters from the violent seas found in the Gulf of Alaska. With more available steam power and maneuvering capability, American steamships began to ply these waters using the pilots of the day.

Among the early Russian pilots was Antonio George Kozian. Formerly in the employ of the Russian American Company, Kozian was known as a "long resident" and "an excellent pilot."[7]

4 Roppel, unpublished notes.

5 Davidson, *Coast Pilot of Alaska*, 124–25.

6 *Pacific Coast Pilot—Alaska, Part 1* (Washington: Government Printing Office, 1883), 160.

7 *Pacific Coast Pilot—Alaska*, 157.

The 1883 *Coast Pilot* notes, "The name would rightly be spelled Kozian."[8]

Although Kozian was the first navigator to report Cozian Reef,[9] he was not the first to discover it. That distinction belongs to the "Russian steamer *Nikolas* [which] struck it [Cozian Reef] in 1854 and it has been called Nikolas Rock."[10]

East Francis Rock and West Francis Rock in Sergius Narrows are named for longtime American pilot Edwin H. Francis. According to Donald Orth, Francis was the first person to make soundings on these rocks.[11] Coming to Sitka in 1868, he eventually operated a small trading steamer in Southeast Alaska. In the 1880s, Francis began piloting government vessels and sailing with the US Coast and Geodetic Survey. He also worked ashore in USGS offices compiling new information and making revisions to the *Alaska Coast Pilot*.[12]

Although the Russians had been using Peril Strait and Olga and Neva Straits for many decades before the Americans arrived, Neva Strait's Whitestone Narrows and Peril Strait's Sergius Narrows were both named by the Americans, in 1869 and in 1895, respectively. A record of Whitestone Narrows is found in the 1883 *Coast Pilot*, in which Captain Meade referred in 1869 to "a reef of white boulders in Neva Strait in mid-channel."

Continuing with his description, Meade wrote, "There is a large rock, which is partly out of the water and right in the center of the channel. The ground is very much broken, and at low water, there is as little as two and one-half fathoms in the channel. By keeping clear of the kelp, which is readily seen, and with the aid of the lead, a vessel of fifteen feet draught can pass through at low

---

8 *Pacific Coast Pilot—Alaska,* 165n.

9 Robert N. DeArmond, "Peril Strait, Part 15, Here and There," *Sitka Sentinel,* February 11, 1999.

10 *Pacific Coast Pilot—Alaska,* 165n.

11 Donald J. Orth, *Dictionary of Alaska Place Names* (US Government Printing Office, 1967), 1038.

12 Roppel, unpublished notes.

water and the largest steamer at high water." Meade called this place Whitestone Narrows.[13]

At Whitestone Narrows on July 2, 1870, at 1200, the USS *Newbern* "stopped to put a buoy on a rock at the southern entrance to 'Neoski Strait' [Neva Strait]. This may have been the first navigation buoy to be placed in Southeast Alaska."[14] The waterway's importance was appreciated early on, and the Americans developed an emerging aid to navigation system for Peril Strait.

In navigating Olga Strait, the 1891 *Coast Pilot* recommended a midchannel course up the strait. "Continue in mid-channel through Olga Strait. About midway in this strait a kelp patch is

13 *Pacific Coast Pilot—Alaska,* 156n.

14 R. N. DeArmond, "Alaska Voyages of USS Newbern The Third, Fourth, and Fifth Voyages: Part II, Conclusion," *The Sea Chest: Journal of the Puget Sound Maritime Historical Society* (September 2002): 20.

The M/V *Matanuska* outbound from Sitka in Olga Strait at Creek Point. PHOTO COURTESY OF CAPTAIN MATTHEW G. WILKENS.

exposed [Middle Shoal] at slack water, making across the surface . . . "[15]

Middle Shoal is not found in the *Dictionary of Alaska Place Names* and was not in official use until the issuance of the 1932 *Coast Pilot*. It was not until January 25, 1938, that a lighted buoy was established on Middle Shoal.[16]

Olga and Neva Straits are both four miles long, but they differ in character. Olga Strait is mostly clear of dangers, other than Middle Shoal, with small flats making out from both sides where streams discharge into the strait.

Neva Strait, however, is rock-infested, requiring careful piloting where very little deviation from a course can be tolerated. The channel limits in Neva Strait are marked by thick kelp in the summer months.

Currents flow parallel to the axis of both straits, but in different directions. For example, the flood current flows northward from Sitka Sound through Olga Strait, meeting the incoming flood current that flows south from Salisbury Sound through Neva Strait to Krestof Sound. During the ebb, the currents separate in Krestof Sound to flow in opposite directions, south through Olga Strait and north through Neva Strait.

The area of Krestof Sound between Olga Point and Neva Point separates Olga Strait from Neva Strait. It was said of this area by Russian authorities that "the tide of Sitka Sound passing from the south meets that which proceeds from the north and produces at times whirls, rips, and choppy cross sea, incommodious to small craft."[17]

Neva Strait was originally described as a narrow channel intermingled with numerous shoals at Whitestone Narrows. Little has changed over the years.

---

15 *Pacific Coast Pilot, Part 1: Dixon Entrance to Yakutat Bay with Inland Passage from Strait of Fuca to Dixon Entrance*, 3rd ed. (Washington: Government Printing Office, 1891), 185.

16 Roppel, unpublished notes.

17 *Pacific Coast Pilot—Alaska*, 153.

> When Neva Strait is well open, head for Whitestone Islet until well up with it; then pass to the eastward of that islet and up the Narrows, steering about midway between the line of Whitestone Islet and the black buoy on one hand and Whitestone Point on the other. Keep on this course until well up to the black [can] buoy[;] then pass between it and the spar buoy on the end of the spit which makes off the eastern shore.[18]

The above 1891 sailing direction is little changed from present-day means of transiting Whitestone Narrows when northbound. As noted in the 1891 *Coast Pilot*, "In June, 1890, the Pacific Coast S/S *Queen*, 341 feet long with a draught of twenty feet when loaded, commanded by Captain James Carroll, made use of this passage without difficulty."[19]

An improved channel, completed in 1959, eliminated the wait for favorable tides. At a price tag of $155,000, the finished project was 200 feet wide and 24 feet deep at mean lower low water through Whitestone Narrows. Whitestone Narrows is the only place along the inside route to Sitka where range lights are found to aid vessels in navigating the center of the narrow channel.

The naming of Sergius Narrows is a more mysterious affair than that of Whitestone Narrows. DeArmond researched this topic for many years, writing the following in a series of exclusive articles on Peril Strait for the *Sitka Sentinel*:

> An example of a place name no longer in use but that can be identified is Brown's Rapids in what is now known as Peril Strait and which can be dated back to at least 1799. In that year, Captain Richard Cleveland came from China to Sitka Sound in the little sloop *Caroline* to buy furs. Years later, he published an account of that voyage and in

18 *Pacific Coast Pilot, Part 1*, 185–86.
19 *Pacific Coast Pilot, Part 1*, 185n.

> it mentions going from Sitka Sound to Chatham Strait and passing through Brown's Rapids.
>
> There were several sea captains named Brown in the early Alaska sea trade, but only one of them had been here before 1799. Captain William Brown commanded the British trading vessels *Butterworth* in 1792 and *Jackal* in 1793. He was killed in the Hawaiian Islands in 1795.
>
> There is little doubt that Brown's Rapids is today known as Sergius Narrows, and it is clear from Captain Cleveland's narrative that the waterway that took him to Chatham Strait was today's Peril Strait.[20]

DeArmond expands this topic:

> Sergius Channel has two different definitions. According to the *Dictionary of Alaska Place Names,* it lies between Pinta Head on Baranof Island, and Sergius Point on Chichagof Island. The channel, as thus described, is cluttered by an island and many rocks and reefs. However, Sergius Channel according to the *US Coast Pilot*, 18th edition, "is a 24-foot deep and 450-foot wide dredged channel that leads through Sergius Narrows."
>
> Both Sergius Point and the original Sergius Channel, according to Orth, were probably named by Comdr. J.B. Coghlan, USN, of the USS *Adams*, in 1884 and appeared in the Coast Pilot in 1895. The point is marked by Sergius Narrows Light . . .
>
> Sergius Narrows, however, was named by Lt. Comdr. E. K. Moore, USN, in 1895.[21] It is odd that a name for this important waterway did not appear on the charts before that. Apparently, the

20 Robert N. DeArmond, "Sitka Names and Places, Around & About Alaska, Notes and Comments," *Sitka Sentinel*, October 22, 1998.

21 Orth, *Dictionary of Alaska Place Names*, 854, 855.

geographers did not find a name on the Russian charts, which they often cited for other names. As I mentioned earlier, in 1799 Captain Richard Cleveland called it Brown's Rapids, but so far as is known he did not put that name on any map or chart.

In 1868 the USS *Saginaw,* [under the command of] Captain Mitchell, went through Peril Strait several times. On June 24, bound from Sitka for Saginaw Bay, at 5:15 a.m. [as logged on *Saginaw* with brevity] "entered Peril Strait. Current too strong. Anchored."

On another voyage, at 10:30 a.m. on July 18, "Passed through Peril Rapids." Later that year, on December 22, the *Saginaw,* bound for Sitka in command of Captain Meade, [logged:] "At 10 a.m. entered Poghibshi Strait [the Russian name for Peril Strait]; at 2:30 passed through the rapids of Lost Strait; 6 p.m. came to in Sitka Harbor."

On another trip through Peril Strait toward Sitka, on January 31, 1869, Captain Meade tried to buck through what he called "the second rapids" but could only have been Sergius Narrows, on a flood tide and came very close to losing his ship. That incident is chronicled in *The USS Saginaw in Alaska Waters*, published by Limestone Press.

None of which answers the question, "Who was Sergius?" It is a common Russian first name, but why did Comdr. Coghlan attach it to these two features? It is possible that he had a Russian with that name aboard as pilot, but the facts are unlikely to be discovered.[22]

22 Robert N. DeArmond, "Peril Strait, Part 7, Around & About Alaska, Notes and Comments," *Sitka Sentinel*, December 10, 1998.

By 1883, the character of these waterways was known and ably described. "The shores are high, wooded and steep—the effect being to render this part of the strait a dark and gloomy gorge, apparently traversed by a torrent."[23]

The 1883 *Coast Pilot* reads, "The western portion [of Peril Strait] is contracted in width, obstructed with numerous dangers, and [also] by the strong and turbulent tidal currents to which it is subject . . . "[24]

"The East and West Francis Rocks, discovered in 1884 . . . are a danger of great magnitude in entering Sergius Channel."[25] It was noted that West Francis Rock was marked by bullwhip kelp and

23 *Pacific Coast Pilot—Alaska,* 163.
24 *Pacific Coast Pilot—Alaska,* 160
25 *Pacific Coast Pilot, Part 1,* 182.

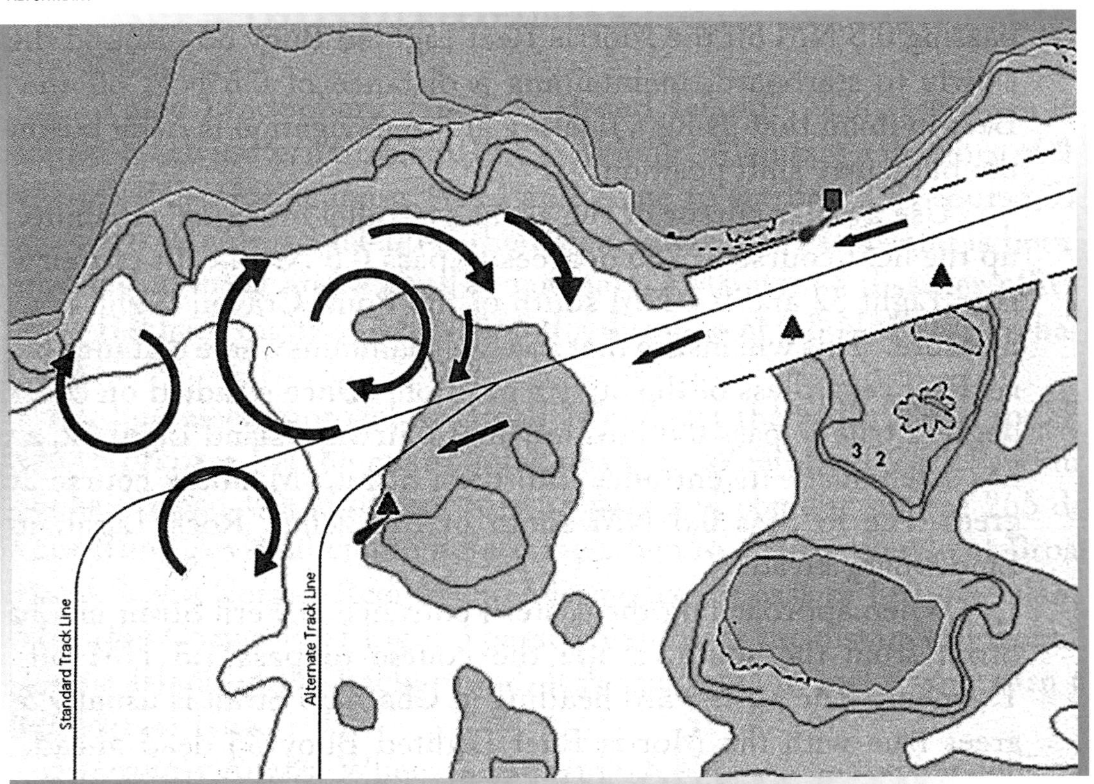

Sergius Narrows Ebb-Current Diagram near West Francis Rock Light Buoy 6. Photo courtesy of Captain Wayne Carnes, computer enhanced by Dale Miller, *UAS-Ketchikan.*

East Francis Rock was not. West Francis Rock Buoy 6 marks West Francis Rock.

Present-day Wayanda Ledge, originally named Eureka Ledge, delineates the southern edge of Sergius Channel, topped by Prolewy Rock. Robert DeArmond calls Wayanda Ledge "a wicked reef on the south side of Sergius Channel. Two red nun buoys mark the edge of the channel. Sergius Narrows Buoy 8 marks an unnamed rock with 16 feet of water over it; Wayanda Ledge Buoy 10 warns of the reef. It was named Wayanda Rock by the Coast & Geodetic Survey for the Revenue Cutter *Wayanda*. That name appeared in the 1883 edition of the *Coast Pilot*. It has also

Sergius Narrows Flood-Current Diagram near Wayanda Ledge Buoy 10. PHOTO COURTESY OF CAPTAIN WAYNE CARNES, COMPUTER ENHANCED BY DALE MILLER, *UAS-KETCHIKAN*.

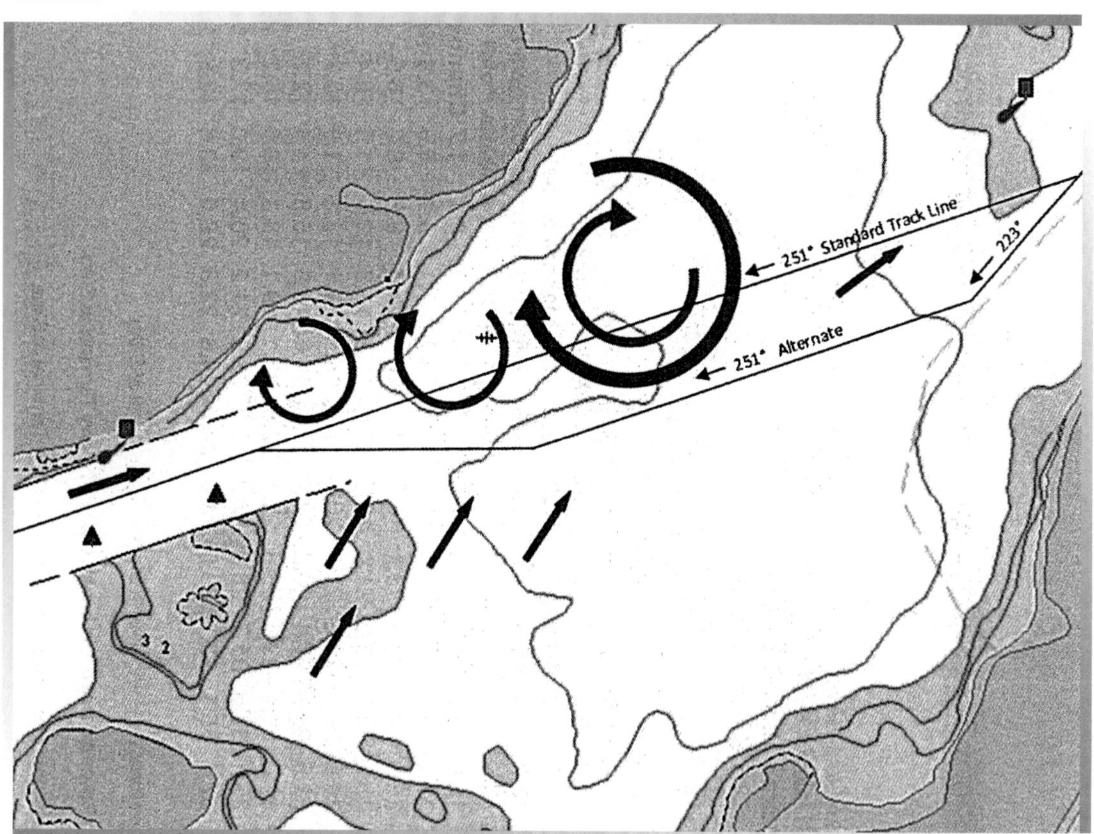

been called Eureka Ledge, for a steamer *Eureka*, and that name appeared on the chart for a time. Both vessels hit the ledge."[26]

Today, Sergius Narrows Buoy 8 and Wayanda Ledge Buoy 10, marking the southern limits of Sergius Channel, are nearly in line with one another while West Francis Rock Buoy 6 is a small distance to the south of the lineup.

"The strong tidal currents here cause rapids, the whirls and eddies of which render it at all times a difficult passage. Vessels always wait for a favorable tide to go through . . . "[27] At strength the flood current sweeps over Wayanda Ledge northeastward, setting strongly across the Sergius Narrows channel diagonally and impinging on the waiting Chichagof Island shore between Sergius Point and Shoal Point. It does not flow parallel with the channel. The 1932 *Coast Pilot* describes the flood current as "heaving up over the ledge."[28] The ebb current flows in a more parallel direction with the channel. Sergius Narrows buoys lean over and submerge under the force of the powerful currents. As the buoys are pulled underwater and struggle to remain afloat, usually in currents 5.0 knots and greater, v-shaped surface streams of current and white froth mark their positions.

Descriptions in the 1891 *Coast Pilot* are vivid. We read with regard to Peril Strait, "For the next 8 miles the navigation is the most dangerous of any in Southeastern Alaska, except Kootznahoo Inlet, owing to the strong tides and sunken rocks that obstruct this passage."[29]

The 1891 *Coast Pilot* reads like a whitewater rafting expedition:

> After passing Suloia Point, Peril Strait turns to the NNW, into the Sergius Channel, which at its narrowest part is scarce[ly] 100 yards in width, and is rendered very dangerous by the sunken rocks

---

26 Robert N. DeArmond, "Peril Strait, Part 8, Around & About Alaska, Notes and Comments," *Sitka Sentinel*, December 17, 1998.

27 *Pacific Coast Pilot—Alaska*, 162.

28 *United States Coast Pilot—Alaska, Part 1: Dixon Entrance to Yakutat Bay*, 8th ed. (Washington: US Government Printing Office, 1932), 398.

29 *Pacific Coast Pilot, Part 1*, 181.

> over which the tide rushes in its strength with the sound of a roaring cataract, the current often running more than 10 knots . . .
>
> The W. shore of Sergius Channel is steep and heavily wooded, with deep water close-to . . . Shoal Point, about 1/3 mile to the NNE of Sergius Point, has a rocky ledge projecting out about 30 yards. A narrow fringe of kelp extends along the shore between these two points. Above Shoal Point the strong current of the channel rapidly diminishes.[30]

The 1932 *Coast Pilot* goes on to warn about current deflections.

> With a strong north-flowing current a sharp deflection occurs at Shoal Point, which is dangerous, especially to long vessels bound southward, as it sheers the bow eastward in the direction of Wayanda Ledge, and there is little room to straighten out again on the proper channel line. With a strong south-flowing current a similar sharp deflection occurs westward of the West Francis Rock, which is dangerous, especially to long vessels, bound either way, as it sheers the bow in toward the cove on the west side.[31]

Before permanent nomenclature was applied, early American *Coast Pilots* called Sergius Narrows the Second or Southern Rapid.

> Rapids Island, and between it and the opposite shore the clear channel is not over a third of a mile in width. From this point [Sergius Point] to Povorotni [Turnabout] Island the strait is more or less contracted and obstructed by islets and rocks, amongst which, at certain states of the tide, a bore,

30 *Pacific Coast Pilot, Part 1,* 182.

31 *Pacific Coast Pilot, Part 1,* 398.

> race or tide-rip is produced of great strength and alarming proportions. This is especially severe at certain of the narrowest places. The race nearest Rapids Island is denominated the Second or Southern Rapid.[32]

We tend to forget that the area of Rapids Point near Rose Channel and opposite from Yellow Point is also an area of extreme current. There is no mention of this fact in modern *Coast Pilot*s. The 1883 *Coast Pilot* calls them the First or Northern Rapids.

"Abreast of Rapids Point the whole strait is less than half a mile in width, and this is diminished nearly one half for navigation by the islets. Hence at this point, at certain stages of the tide, the so-called First or Northern Rapid is formed, consisting of a race of great force and velocity. At spring tides it is said to attain a velocity of ten knots an hour."[33]

By the time of publication of the 1891 *Coast Pilot*, the First or Northern Rapids had lost their name and diminished in importance. This edition notes that "tide swirls are quite strong off this point (Yellow Point) during its strongest flow,"[34] and that these "sometimes take charge of the vessel."[35] The 1891 authors correctly recommended the nearby Adams Channel leading around Big Rose and Little Rose Islands as the preferred channel over the narrower Rose Channel.

Rounding Big Rose and Little Rose Islands is very nearly a 90-degree course change. This reach is accurately described as "a broad, safe channel, and the tides, though strong, are less objectionable."[36] These islands were originally named the Opasni [dangerous] Islets or Peril Islets, according to the 1883 *Coast Pilot*.

Most vessels transiting Peril Strait do so to arrive at Sergius Narrows near a period of slack water. Few see the currents at full strength. The Alaska Marine Highway System's high-speed ferry,

---

32 *Pacific Coast Pilot—Alaska,* 161.
33 *Pacific Coast Pilot—Alaska,* 163.
34 *Pacific Coast Pilot, Part 1,* 183.
35 *Pacific Coast Pilot, Part 1,* 187.
36 *Pacific Coast Pilot, Part 1,* 183.

Rounding Big Rose Island at Rose Island Rock Light 19. PHOTO COURTESY OF CAPTAIN MATTHEW G. WILKENS.

FVF *Fairweather*, however, traverses Peril Strait regardless of the current. Captain Wayne Carnes, master of the FVF *Fairweather*, comments about the First or Northern Rapids between Rapids Point and Yellow Point:

> It is this area where we experience very strong turbulence that is commonly stronger than what we see in Sergius Narrows—back eddies, upwelling, and whirlpools. On more than one occasion, we have seen fifty-to-eighty-foot fishing vessels nearly roll over while they transit this area during strong currents. The *Fairweather* gets pushed around, but there is decent sea room (it is all relative) and the ship is easily kept on track.[37]

37 Captain Wayne Carnes, Alaska Marine Highway System, personal unpublished piloting notes on Peril Strait and Sergius Narrows, Juneau, Alaska, December 15, 2006.

Modern ships can be powerful instruments with twin diesel engines, twin rudders, variable pitch propellers, and omnidirectional bow thrusters. Thus, it can be tempting to bulldoze through these turbulent currents.

In the summer of 1984, when the Jetfoil *Ares* was being tested by the Alaska Marine Highway System, Captain Jeff Baken "observed an 80′ seine boat caught in a huge whirlpool about 150′ in diameter and with a vertical [drop] of about 10′ from the outer edge into the deep center. The seine boat was completely caught, spinning uncontrollably, while the fishermen waved haplessly from the flying bridge."[38]

Always remember that a current's set or direction must be considered and that the calculated strength of the current is only a prediction. Assume that the forces arrayed against a vessel are stronger than they actually are, thereby avoiding an accident. A prudent shipmaster will time the transit of Sergius Narrows to fall within a half-hour window on either side of the predicted time of slack water.

Povorotni Island is a key point of geography in Peril Strait. Here, the broader eastern reaches of Peril Strait meet the narrow western reaches. Ensign Vasiliev of the Russian Navy named Povorotni Island in 1833. It means to turn about a "point or pivot, around or about which one turns in passing."[39] Indeed, the turn at Povorotni is also a nearly 90-degree course change. However, it also could have served as a double meaning, warning sailing vessels to stand clear of Peril Strait.

Povorotni Island was known as Canoe Island for a time between 1835 and 1875. A footnote in the 1883 *Coast Pilot* explains, "This islet was conspicuously marked by a canoe, which indicated the burial place of a family of Sitka Indians who died of measles in 1835."[40]

Hoggatt Reefs are extensive, rising to low-lying and grass-covered Hoggatt Island. They are located 2.7 nautical miles

---

38 Captain Jeff Baken, email correspondence, January 2, 2019.

39 *Pacific Coast Pilot—Alaska,* 162.

40 *Pacific Coast Pilot—Alaska,* 163.

northeast of Povorotni Island. No record of vessel groundings can be found here, but at high tide Hoggatt Island can cover and disappear from sight. In times of reduced visibility, high water, or high wind, the island can be hard to find even with radar. In the early 1980s, the crew of the M/V *Malaspina* placed a homemade structure with a day beacon on Hoggatt Reefs. This was later followed by an official light, which the US Coast Guard placed on the southernmost rock of Hoggatt Reefs to better mark this dangerous location. This is perhaps one of the newest aids to navigation to be established in Peril Strait.

Nearby Otstoia Passage is a local name, not an official name, given to the very narrow passageway found between Otstoia Island, Cozian Reef, and Nismeni Point, the northernmost point of Baranof Island. *Otstoia* is a Russian word meaning "distant," and some had called the island Distant Island. Adds Robert DeArmond, "There is a steamboat channel with about 7 fathoms of water between Otstoia Island and the Baranof Island shore, but it is constricted to a clear width of 150 yards by an extensive flat on the Baranof Island side."[41] This short waterway was once considered the main channel for all vessels.

The 1883 *Coast Pilot* says:

> Between Otstoia Island and the shore is a passage which was principally made use of by Russian navigators. It is about two and half cables [0.25 NM] over all, and the half of this near the Baranof shore is occupied by the bank or shoal which here fringes the coast. In the channel close to the island eight and ten fathoms of water may be had and there are no obstructions. Though very narrow, this passage appears to have been preferred by the Russian traders, whether as better known, freer from strong currents or otherwise, is nowhere recorded.[42]

---

41 DeArmond, "Peril Strait, Part 15."

42 *Pacific Coast Pilot—Alaska,* 164.

It remains a mystery why the passage is not officially named on nautical charts. Neither is Otstoia Passage found in the *Dictionary of Alaska Place Names.* The channel's use, however, has been outlined in all editions of *Farwell's Hansen Handbook* as the main passageway. "There is a shipping channel on each side of Otstoia Island," wrote DeArmond. "Neither channel has a name on today's charts and the reason for this is unclear."

DeArmond continues, "In 1876 the U.S. Collector of Customs at Sitka referred to the channel east of Otstoia Island as Newbern Channel and the one to the west as Saginaw Channel. The Coast and Geodetic Survey did not pick up on the names . . . The channel on the west side of Otstoia Island is the wider and deeper of the two."[43]

There was some folklore concerning the waters west of Otstoia Island and Otstoia Passage. Steve Pierce of Petersburg recounted working on a cannery tender that used Otstoia Passage regularly.

> I knew there were tricky spots in Peril Strait, but nobody ever mentioned Otstoia Passage. After clearing Otstoia Island, I asked the skipper, "Why do we go through there?"
>
> The skipper replied, "I just think it is safer. If you mess up going through [inside Otstoia Island], you have a 50% chance of hitting a sand beach. If you mess up out there [outside Otstoia Island], you have a 100% chance of hitting a rock."[44]

This may also be a reflection of the Russian thinking. However, some who use the channel point out that it is 0.90 NM shorter in distance than using the longer route north of Otstoia Passage. The longer route north of Otstoia Island has been surveyed and is well charted. It is found to be mostly deep, very wide, and clear of any dangers, dispelling any notions of unwarranted hazards. Today, the main route used by most navigators passes near Broad Island

43 DeArmond, "Peril Strait, Part 15."

44 Steve Pierce, email correspondence, March 31, 2007.

and outside Elovoi and Krugloi Islands, avoiding Otstoia Passage entirely.

Indeed, the modern route passes near Broad Island to be well clear and beyond Otstoia Island and Cozian Reef. In 1833, Russian Ensign Vasiliev named this Poperechni Island, meaning "across" or "on the other side or transverse,"[45] most likely with regard to Otstoia Island and Passage. Poperechni was "mistranslated as Broad Island on some charts,"[46] perhaps because of the 2.10 NM broadness of water separating this island from Otstoia Island.

Lying in wait under that serene broadness is Cozian Reef. Extending for nearly three-quarters of a mile northeast from the northeast end of Otstoia Island with a least depth of 1.5 feet, the reef's easternmost end is marked by Cozian Reef Light 3. Robert DeArmond writes, "The reef was named in 1880 by the U.S. Navy, in other words, by someone from the USS *Jamestown*, stationed at Sitka—for Antonio George Cozian, a pilot who had been in the service of the Russian American Company. He was said to have first reported it."

DeArmond continues:

> In 1875 George Cozian was skipper on the trading schooner *Nellie Edes*, owned by a Sitka merchant, William Phillipson. While returning to Sitka from a voyage, the schooner struck Cozian Reef, and that may have been when he reported the reef, although the Russian steamboat *Nicolai* is said to have struck there in 1854.
>
> The *Nellie Edes* was not much damaged[,] but the 413-ton mail steamer *Gussie Telfair* which hit the reef on October 30, 1876, was less fortunate. She managed to get off the rocks and reach Sitka where she was put on the beach. Repairs required five days.[47]

45 *Pacific Coast Pilot—Alaska,* 165; Orth, *Dictionary of Alaska Place Names,* 161.

46 *Pacific Coast Pilot—Alaska,* 165n.

47 DeArmond, "Peril Strait, Part 15."

Perhaps no stories of vessel accidents in Peril Strait are more coincidental or convoluted than those of the Revenue Cutter *Wayanda* and the mail steamer *Eureka*. Robert DeArmond recounted them in detail.

On May 14, 1868, the Revenue Cutter *Wayanda,* under the command of Captain J. W. White, touched a ledge in Sergius Narrows that now carries the name Wayanda Ledge. Then, on January 6, 1869, the *Wayanda,* again under the command of Captain White, struck a rock in Tongass Narrows known for a time as Wayanda Rock. After a second ship, the steamer *California,* struck it, the rock was given its present-day name of California Rock.

Wayanda was sold in 1873 to the Pacific Coast Steamship Company and renamed *Los Angeles.* In 1881, the *California* was sold and renamed *Eureka.* On April 26, 1883, the *Eureka,* under the command of Captain J. C. Hunter,[48] scraped Wayanda Ledge, opening up its side and leaking badly. The steamer was purposefully grounded nearby, and the passengers and crew were rescued.

Both the *Los Angeles* (ex-*Wayanda*) and the *Eureka* (ex-California) are the only two vessels known to have struck both Wayanda Ledge in Sergius Narrows and California Rock in Tongass Narrows.[49]

There is a record of some spectacular maritime accidents in Peril Strait, Neva Strait, and Olga Strait. Although Wrangell Narrows near Petersburg is far narrower and noted to be one of Alaska's most accident-prone waterways, Peril Strait has taken its toll as well. In the lengthy history of the Alaska Marine Highway System, a greater number of serious accidents have occurred in Peril Strait than in Wrangell Narrows.

---

48 Captain J. C. Hunter was a popular and much-celebrated vessel master in Alaska. In his lengthy career, he was involved with the wrecks of the S/S *Umatilla* near Port Townsend, Washington, in 1896 and the S/S *Farallon* at Illiamna Bay, Alaska, on January 5, 1910. See Steve K. Lloyd, *Farallon Shipwreck and Survival on the Alaskan Shore* (Washington State University Press, 2000) and Pennelope J. Goforth, *Sailing the Mail in Alaska* (Anchorage: CybrrCat Publications, 2003).

49 DeArmond, "Peril Strait, Part 8, Around & About Alaska," *Sitka Sentinel*, December 17, 1998.

There is no ready explanation for this phenomenon, but there has been some speculation that because Peril Strait is wider in most instances than Wrangell Narrows, navigators might let their guard down.

Wrangell Narrows can be intense, with "rocks right outside the window." Peril Strait, however, can seem less demanding for a pilot used to the tighter waterways of Southeastern Alaska. There is always the present danger of a mechanical difficulty, and as another shipmaster once said, "When that happens, your goose is cooked." Peril Strait, with its numerous rocks, reefs, shoals, and strong currents, has proven to be an unforgiving adversary for any mechanical difficulties, navigational missteps, inattention, or poor judgment.

The first year and a half of operation for the Alaska Marine Highway System, beginning on January 22, 1963, was fraught with difficulty in Peril Strait.

- On June 8, 1963, "the *Malaspina,* while going with the tide north of Sitka and making 22 knots, scraped bottom in Olga Strait with no apparent damage. On June 15, the Captain involved in the *Malaspina* episode was relieved of duty. No reason was given, but he had, among other things, been critical of the system's scheduling and time allotted between ports." Marine Highway lore notes that this master had been invited to have lunch with the port captain in Juneau, and was summarily dismissed after the lunch was concluded.[50]
- "The *Matanuska* scraped bottom on a rock ledge in early September [1964] while rounding Sergius Point, 25 miles north of Sitka. Divers at [Petersburg] discovered a split and bent plate."[51]

  Passenger Clark Davis was a child heading back to school in Ketchikan at the time: "I was sitting in the snack bar when the whole ship shuddered. I looked over the rail and could not

50 Clinton H. Betz, "The Alaska Marine Highway, 1948–1989," *The Sea Chest: Journal of the Puget Sound Maritime Historical Society* 26, no. 2 (1992): 57.

51 Betz, "The Alaska Marine Highway, 1948–1989," 57.

see any water, only boulders and trees. We put on life jackets while the jukebox played 'Tie Me Kangaroo Down, Sport.' They stopped the ship, but we continued on to Petersburg, where we remained for twenty-four hours for an inspection with divers."[52]

- "On January 26, 1964, the *Malaspina* struck Cozian Reef in Peril Strait while inbound to Sitka, making it necessary to travel to Seattle for repairs. A small hole in the bow, cracked plates, and a bent propeller were the result. Todd Shipyard replaced all the keel plates from stem to stern at a cost of $100,000. Strangely, the mate on duty was cleared of negligence because it was dark at the time of the accident. The vessel was traveling about 8–10 knots with a flood tide."[53]
- "On May 30 [1964] the *Matanuska* rammed the troller *Lare* of Kake, in Whitestone Narrows, ten miles north of Sitka. The troller received some damage but was able to proceed under her own power to Sitka."[54]

A rocky start for the Alaska Marine Highway System was followed by eight years of quiet. During this period of quiescence, there is perhaps no stranger story of Peril Strait than that told by Robert DeArmond:

> The winter watchman at Chatham [Sitkoh Bay] in January 1969 was the first to learn of a grim struggle for survival that had taken place off Morris Reef. The tug *Acme*, [skippered by] Captain Harold Hofstad, was towing a barge from Sitka to Seattle. As the tug approached Morris Reef, seaman George Jones called mate Frank Johnson to the side of the vessel and pointed to something in the distance. As Johnson strained his eyes to see what Jones had pointed to, Jones seized him

52 Clark Davis, telephone conversation, Ketchikan, Alaska, January 2004.

53 Betz, "The Alaska Marine Highway, 1948–1989," 58.

54 Betz, "The Alaska Marine Highway, 1948–1989," 59.

> and threw him overboard. Jones then called to the other seaman, Jack Snyder, to come out of the pilothouse. Snyder saw Johnson in the water and yelled, "Johnson, overboard."
>
> Captain Hofstad stopped the tug and started to launch a skiff. Jones grabbed him from behind and tried to dump him overboard, but Hofstad hung onto the mast stay and yelled to Snyder to hit Jones. Snyder grabbed a fire axe and beat Jones to the deck. Johnson had been in the cold water for 15 minutes and was nearly unconscious by the time Hofstad reached him and the skiff nearly swamped as Johnson was hauled aboard. Then Snyder was heard yelling for help. When he got back aboard the *Acme*, Hofstad found that Jones had revived and was trying to put Snyder overboard. The captain beat Jones unconscious with a pipe wrench and tied him up, [and] then headed for Chatham. There the watchman made a radio call and the Alaska Coastal Airlines plane stopped and took Jones to the hospital in Juneau. The tug continued on its way to Seattle.[55]

Strange happenings resumed, haunting navigators of all variety in Peril Strait.

- On September 27, 1972, the 195-ton vessel *Tradewind* burned at Sergius Narrows. No other details are given.[56]
- In 1974, the Alaska Marine Highway System's *Columbia*

> struck West Francis Rock in Peril Strait on October 15 while southbound to Sitka. Choppy seas, high winds, and tidal currents were worse than usual

55 Robert N. DeArmond, "Peril Strait, Part 30, Around and About Alaska," *Sitka Sentinel*, May 27, 1999.

56 *Tradewind*: http://www.mms.gov/alaska/ref/ships/shipdb/searchcause2.asp, accessed February 8, 2005.

> at the time. The starboard hull was ripped open for 100 feet; there was even some rock lodged in the hull.
>
> The *Columbia* was taken to a nearby bay where the damage was assessed and a determination made to proceed to Sitka. The ferry was leaking oil from a ruptured fuel tank. Upon the ferry's arrival at Sitka, [a] containment boom was immediately placed around the vessel. The *LeConte* was sent to Sitka to pick up the *Columbia*'s passengers and take them on to Juneau.[57]

A complex chain of events had preceded the accident. A drilling and blasting outfit had been hired by the US Army Corps of Engineers to widen the western end of Sergius Narrows by removing the pinnacles from West Francis Rock. Following a fire on their barge, the blasting firm reported to the Coast Guard that the pinnacles had been removed. A wire drag was not conducted to confirm the claim, and the Coast Guard pulled the West Francis Rock buoy from the channel.

Coming through the narrows on a dark and rainy night, the *Columbia* had changed her course early where the buoy had once been. Instead of finding a clear passage, the *Columbia* found the pinnacles of West Francis Rock.

Ellis Lundin, the *Columbia*'s long-standing bos'n, remembered:

> It hit forward and tore about eighty feet of hull. It jammed with such force that the rock broke off and lodged in the hull. The *Columbia* had a full load of cars and passengers when this happened. Fortunately, only the ship was damaged. They off-loaded everybody in Sitka and we had to take the vessel clear to Seattle to get the rock out.

57 Betz, "The Alaska Marine Highway, 1948–1989," 66.

> Some divers went down later and found four more pinnacles that the Corps of Engineers had paid this outfit to remove. They got a hold of the Coast Guard, and the next day the buoy was back in place.

It has been in place ever since.

Lundin continued:

> In Seattle, they tried to jackhammer the rock, to bust it up so they could get it out. It was solid granite, and they couldn't get their jackhammers in far enough, so they burned a big hole in the hull of the ship and let the rock fall out on the dry dock.
>
> I have the top of one of those pinnacles. It's a big rock, no doubt about that. The port captain told me to take care of it, so I put it on a pallet board, got it on a trailer, brought it to Ketchikan, and hid it. It's not much of a secret, though, everyone in Ketchikan knows where it is.[58]

Ellis Lundin's memento of West Francis Rock now rests in his yard on the shores of the eastern channel of Tongass Narrows, south of Ketchikan, very close to California Rock. Weighing over a ton, it is scarred with jackhammer holes from the attempt to dislodge it from *Columbia*'s hull.

This sample of West Francis Rock is coarse to the touch yet smooth and somewhat waterworn from eons of tidal currents flowing over it, giving the ancient rock a patina of varnish. In touch and appearance, it has a high factor of hardness. "When the rock was fresh in 1974, we noticed that it was a clean rock without any barnacle growth," added Lundin.

- On May 26, 1975, a USCG cutter was southbound at Big Rose Island, practicing fog navigation, when it overshot the sharp

58 Sharon Bushnell, "Southeast Mariner, Ellis Lundin," *Anchorage Daily News*, August 22, 2004.

Big Rose turn and skimmed the edge of the shoal at the mouth of Range Creek on Baranof Island, directly opposite Big Rose Island. The ship slid to a stop in the soft mud, remaining upright. However, the vessel had a rounded bottom, and the tide was falling rapidly. The crew went ashore, cut some timbers from the woods, and used them to shore up the vessel, saving it from rolling over. The mystery cutter was refloated with tugboat assistance on the next flood tide. Damage was said to be moderate.

A dramatic photo of this grounding hangs in the Pioneer Bar, a popular fishermen's lair on the Sitka waterfront. Patrons cannot read the name on the cutter, but some say it was the buoy tender *Planetree*. Others say it was the *Clover* or one of the faster and smaller patrol boats.

Robert DeArmond writes, "*Clover* arrived at Sitka on July 1, 1965, to replace the *Sorrel*. *Clover* finally left Sitka fifteen years later on January 5, 1980, and thus was in that area all of the 1970s. She is thus a candidate for the grounding in Peril Strait, but is not convicted."[59] Coast Guard historians would not disclose the name, but the vessel in the photograph is larger than a patrol boat and is presumably the USCG cutter *Clover*.

- On June 21, 1975, the Alaska Marine Highway System's M/V *Malaspina* was overtaking the inbound F/V *Forester* in Olga Strait, when at the last moment the fishing vessel turned to pass under the bow of the advancing *Malaspina*. A collision followed, and the *Forester* sank. Tragically, the operator of the *Forester* died in the accident.[60]

- On September 7, 1980, the tugboat *Neoga* caught on fire in Olga Strait near Olga Point. The rupture of a hydraulic oil line, spraying oil onto the hot engine manifold and igniting the oil, had caused the fire. The *Neoga* was burned beyond repair and

59 Robert DeArmond, personal correspondence, Sitka, Alaska, August 24, 2007.

60 *Forester*: http://www.mms.gov/alaska/ref/ships/shipdb/searchcause2.asp, accessed February 8, 2005.

remains to this day a rusting hulk beached on the shore at Halleck Point.[61]

- On February 10, 1982, the Alaska Marine Highway System's M/V *Aurora* was running late on the flood tide while inbound to Sitka from Kake. Low water slack was at 1942 (7:42 p.m.) Pacific Standard Time,[62] and the *Aurora* arrived at Sergius Narrows at 2013 (8:13 p.m.), thirty-one minutes after low water slack. It was barely one minute past the time window for safely doing so.

  The best helmsman was placed on the wheel, and it was decided to run the narrows. Going against the 3.4-knot strength of a gathering 6.9-knot flood current, the helmsman exercised the rudder to maintain the course, rolling the ship from side to side, as though buffeted by a strong wind.

  Between Shoal Point and Sergius Point, the rudder became unresponsive and stuck on 10° right. Switching to the non-follow-up system (NFU), a backup steering system, failed to generate a response despite there being electrical power to it. The failure lasted long enough for the ship to sheer toward Sergius Point. With full astern on both engines, the captain was able to stop the ship before striking the rocky shore at Sergius Point. However, while backing, the ship gained sternway.

  It backed away from Sergius Point but parallel to the shore, rather than toward the center of the channel. It is believed the diagonally flowing flood current's set pinned the *Aurora* close to the Chichagof Island shore, preventing it from coming farther into the deeper water of the channel. As the vessel continued backing to clear Shoal Point, the underwater stern directly hit a small detached, submerged rock lurking

61 *Neoga*: http://www.mms.gov/alaska/ref/ships/shipdb/searchcause2.asp, accessed February 8, 2005.

62 Most contemporary computerized tide programs give times in Alaska Standard Time for the year 1982. Before 1983, the legal time zone for Southeastern Alaska was Pacific Standard Time (UTC-8). In 1983, Alaska's state government put most of Alaska, including Southeastern Alaska, on the Alaska Standard Time (UTC-9) time zone, one hour earlier than Pacific Standard Time.

immediately offshore Shoal Point, marked on the chart as "PA" or position approximate.

As a result, *Aurora* lost both rudders. One rudderpost snapped cleanly, flush with the hull, and the other fell out entirely from the rudder yoke in the steering engine room. Both propeller shafts were bent and the fix-bladed propellers mangled, with all blades bent forward, rendering the ship unmaneuverable. These rudders remain somewhere on the bottom of Sergius Narrows.

The *Aurora* drifted out of control in the flood current northward of Liesnoi Shoal to Middle Rock, where the captain was able to drop its single anchor in 25 fathoms (150 feet) of water. However, the anchor dragged in a stiff northerly wind over poor holding ground. As a result, *Aurora* nearly grounded a second time on Middle Rock but was saved just as the tugboat *Lutak Pride* arrived from Sitka early the next morning at 0020 (12:20 a.m.) to attach a soft towline to the bow.

The next morning at daylight, the *Aurora* was towed to Ushk Bay, northwest of Povorotni Island in lower Hoonah Sound, where all the passengers were safely transferred to the M/V *Taku* in lifeboats. The *Aurora* was then inspected by a marine insurance inspector and towed to Auke Bay, north of Juneau, where an initial Coast Guard inquiry was made.[63] Following the inquiry, the stricken vessel was sent to Seattle for a lengthy repair, towed the entire distance by the tugboat *Leonard M* out of Wrangell. Once safely in a Seattle dry dock, *Aurora* awaited new rudders and propellers, which had to be manufactured from scratch using the original blueprints.

Following a lengthy accident investigation, it was discovered that vibrations had twisted loose a small screw. It had rolled around on a horizontal steering stand circuit board, causing an electrical short and the initial reason for the rudder not responding to the helmsman. Had it not been for the

63 Per logbook of the M/V *Aurora*, February 10–19, 1982, Alaska State Archives, Juneau, Alaska.

loose screw, the *Aurora* would have made it through Sergius Narrows without incident. The Coast Guard later exonerated the *Aurora*'s captain and crew. (Circuit boards today are inserted vertically.)[64]

Passenger Sonya M. Smith of Hoonah never forgot the experience, as she wrote in the *Juneau Empire*:

> I recall being on the *Aurora* when it ran aground in Peril Straits. I know at that time it was attributed to a steering failure. I remember the chaos it caused as it was night and the tide through the Straits ran like a wild river. I remember seeing blue sparks [bioluminescence] glowing in the water and an awful shudder as the propeller was hitting the beach. We were able to pull off and anchor off shore; awaiting evacuation to another vessel. I remember not wanting to give up my life vest even though the crew announced that [life vests] were no longer necessary.
>
> Come daylight we were herded into lifeboats off the back end of the *Aurora* and through choppy waters headed to the *Taku* where we were lifted aboard and taken to Juneau. We were treated very well by the crews of both vessels. It is a memory that I will not soon forget.[65]

- On May 3, 1983, the Alaska Marine Highway System's M/V *Columbia* struck Haley Rocks in Fish Bay. The ship was outbound from Sitka while waiting for a log tow to clear Sergius Narrows as it rode the beginning of an ebb tide. *Columbia* conducted a series of slow round turns in Fish Bay as it waited. However, with each turn the ebb current slowly set the *Columbia* to the south and closer to the submerged and unmarked Haley Rocks. The *Columbia*'s set apparently went

---

64 Author's personal recollections (I was the second mate on board the M/V *Aurora* but off-duty the night of this incident).

65 Sonya M. Smith, Letter to the Editor, *Juneau Empire*, May 16, 2004.

unnoticed by the crew. As the ship came about to line up for Sergius Narrows, it struck Haley Rocks along the port side. Some 210 feet of shell plating was damaged and dimpled.

"Who discovered [Haley Rocks] is not known," writes Robert DeArmond, "but one of the State ferries rediscovered them a short while back while circling to wait for the tide in Sergius Narrows. The Coast Guard let the skipper know that it was not pleased."[66]

To this day, Haley Rocks remain unmarked by any light, buoy, or daymark. Although Haley Rocks show kelp in the summer, in the winter there is no kelp to mark the position of the rocks. When in the area of Fish Bay, keep Haley Rocks in mind.

- On April 10, 1986, the tugboat *Roughneck* sank in Sergius Narrows as it pulled the unwieldy barge *Annahootz*. Earlier on this same disastrous voyage, the *Roughneck* and the *Annahootz* had fetched up on an unnamed sandspit extending into the channel from Mitkof Island behind Light 32 in Wrangell Narrows. The *Annahootz*, carrying a load of fuel and freight, had yawed strongly from side to side while northbound through Wrangell Narrows. The barge had veered out of the narrow channel, dragging the underpowered, single-screw *Roughneck* along and grounding both on the spit. The crew was able to resume their voyage at high tide.

  Later, as the *Roughneck* approached Sergius Narrows on the night of April 10, it slowed down to navigate the narrow channel while going against a flood current, but the unpredictable barge *Annahootz* failed to slow down. While yawing forcefully on the short towline, it tripped the tugboat, pulling the R*oughneck* over and sinking it to the bottom of Sergius Narrows.[67]

---

66 DeArmond, "Peril Strait, Part 7."

67 Brian A. Chinell, a survivor of the tugboat *Roughneck* sinking in Sergius Narrows, Sitka, Alaska.

There were two fatalities and three fortunate survivors. Today, the *Roughneck* rests on the bottom of Sergius Narrows in 20 fathoms (120 feet) of water near Shoal Point. It is marked with a wreck symbol on the nautical chart, and vessels navigating the narrows pass over the top of the wreckage.

- On August 18, 1988, the fishing tender *Melissa Chris* capsized and was later raised in Peril Strait. No other details are given.[68]
- In February 1999, the Alaska Marine Highway System vessel M/V *Taku* was passing eastbound off Rodman Bay in Peril Strait through afternoon curtains of heavy snow showers. A turbo shaft to the main generator broke, spewing atomized oil directly into the generator exhaust stack. The oil ignited in the hot gas plume, becoming a blowtorch. Although flames did not issue from the stack, volumes of white smoke erupted. Generator stack metal became white-hot. Thankfully, thick wrappings of stack insulation prevented the spreading of intense heat from the fire.

  A passenger muster was taken, and lifeboats were prepared for lowering. The *Taku* slowed down to idle speed, hugging the Chichagof Island shore to be near good landing beaches near False Island. The generator was shut down, putting the fire out. It took some time to discover the initial source of the fire. A second generator was placed online, and *Taku* resumed her voyage to Juneau.[69]
- In August 1999, the Alaska Marine Highway System's outbound M/V *LeConte* had a near collision with the inbound high-speed cruise vessel *Spirit of Endeavor* in dense fog near Big Island, northeast of Sergius Narrows. The vessels came within 30 yards of each other and only seconds from what could have been a devastating collision. Coast Guard investigators found no appreciable negligence in the case.

68 *Melissa Chris*: http://www.mms.gov/alaska/ref/ships/shipdb/searchcause2.asp, accessed February 8, 2005.

69 Captain Scott Macaulay, personal recollections, Juneau, Alaska, March 2007.

- On January 26, 2004, while made up alongside a 300-foot container barge loaded with 200 container vans, the tug *Corbin Foss* lost control of its engines. *Corbin Foss*'s pneumatic controls had ceased to function due to frozen moisture in the control lines that had been exposed to a temperature of 15° Fahrenheit. A cold wind was blowing out of Katlian Bay, setting the *Corbin Foss* and her barge toward Little Gavanski Island and Border Rocks.

  At the time, the Alaska Marine Highway's M/V *Aurora* was inbound at nearby Dog Point to the ferry terminal at Starrigavan Bay. Hearing the *Corbin Foss*'s distress call, the *Aurora* rendered assistance. By placing *Aurora*'s bow near a corner of the drifting barge and passing first a heaving line and then a mooring line to the *Corbin Foss*'s seamen, the rescuers were able to attach their vessel to the barge.

  With a mooring line secured to the barge, the *Aurora* placed its engines astern, putting a strain on the mooring line to stop the drift of the *Corbin Foss* and its barge. The *Aurora* continued pulling the *Corbin Foss* and its barge by going astern into nearby Starrigavan Bay. The tug *Western Mariner* then took over, and the ferry completed its voyage to the ferry terminal. A Coast Guard commendation was issued to the *Aurora* and its crew for their fast actions.[70]

- On May 10, 2004, 150 years after the discovery grounding of the Russian steamer *Nikolas*, the Alaska Marine Highway System vessel M/V *LeConte* grounded on Cozian Reef while attempting to transit Otstoia Passage. "The grounding caused $3 million in damage. The cause of the grounding was determined to be operator error, not tidal currents."[71]

  The *LeConte* had suffered a great amount of damage to its underwater hull, to the extent that it sank on the reef. Eighty-six passengers, twenty-three crewmembers, and fifteen

70 Captain Scott Macaulay, personal recollections, Juneau, Alaska, March 2007.

71 See http://en.wikipedia.org/wiki/Peril_Strait

vehicles were onboard.[72] Crew and passengers abandoned the ship in lifeboats, injuring one passenger as the lifeboats were lowered to the water.

Due to the shallow but uneven depth of Cozian Reef, 1.5 feet to 60 feet,[73] *LeConte* was held precariously upright and could not submerge below the surface of the sea. After a vigorous salvage effort that included temporary patches to the hull in five compartments, *LeConte* was saved. Twenty-three thousand gallons of fuel and fifteen vehicles were also safely removed from the listing vessel.[74]

The sunken vessel was refloated one week later, on May 17. Under tow with tugboat escort for 263 nautical miles, the wounded *LeConte* arrived safely at the Alaska Ship and Dry Dock shipyard in Ketchikan three days later. Once in the dry dock and lifted from the water, the ship had 90,000 pounds of damaged steel replaced.

The National Transportation Safety Board concluded that crew fatigue due to significant sleep deficit led to lack of awareness for the location of Cozian Reef.[75]

- On October 21, 2005, the *Anchorage Daily News* reported, "A 28-foot humpback whale washed up dead in Peril Strait near Sitka last weekend with wounds that suggest a ship smashed into its head, according to scientists who examined the carcass on Tuesday. A necropsy found extensive hemorrhaging and bleeding along the whale's lower right jaw."[76] This incident occurred between Fairway Island and McClellan Rock.

---

72 See http://en.wikipedia.org/wiki/Peril_Strait

73 *United States Coast Pilot 8, Pacific Coast of Alaska: Dixon Entrance to Cape Spencer* (Washington, DC: US Department of Commerce, National Oceanic and Atmospheric Administration, 1990), 210.

74 Rick Janelle, *Unified Command After Action Report,* M/V *LECONTE Response,* Marine Safety Office, US Coast Guard, Juneau, Alaska, May 21, 2004.

75 Marine Accident Brief, *Accident Number DCA-04-MM-020,* National Transportation Safety Board, Washington, DC.

76 Doug O'Harra, "Whale Likely Killed in Collision with Boat," *Anchorage Daily News,* October 21, 2005, p. B1.

Peril Strait

General

General

Securité Calls on VHF Channels 13 and 16

- When inbound for Peril Strait and Sitka, give a Securité call after making the turn at Hoggatt Reef Light 25. Transit time to Sergius Narrows is approximately 45 minutes.
- Give a second Sergius Narrows Securité call between Big Island and Point Siroi if necessary due to reduced visibility.
- When inbound via Neva Strait, give a Securité call at Kane Island for Whitestone Narrows. Transit time from Kane Island to Whitestone Narrows is approximately 20 minutes.
- When outbound, give a Securité call for Whitestone Narrows upon departure from the Alaska State Ferry Terminal. Transit time to Whitestone Narrows is approximately 40 minutes.
- If outbound in reduced visibility, give a second Securité call for Whitestone Narrows at Creek Point. From here, transit time to Whitestone Narrows is approximately 10 minutes.
- When outbound, give a Securité call for Sergius Narrows when at Scraggy Island, north of Kane Island. From Scraggy Island to Sergius Narrows, transit time is approximately 15 minutes.
- When making Securité calls on channel 13, make sure to use the full-power mode instead of 1 watt so that the signal can span the entire length of the narrows.
- Always respond to a vessel that has given a Securité call that is of concern to you. Remember that "concerned traffic" is

traffic that can report visibility and traffic conditions, even though such traffic may not meet your vessel directly.

Radar Range Scales

- For navigating Peril Strait, the ¾-mile radar range scale is the best for good resolution and for seeing ahead to the next course change. For some of the more open and longer reaches, the 1½-mile range scale is more useful.
- It is most advantageous to have the sweep at the center of the scope so that the outer scale can be used as a quick reference to determine either a bearing or the next course to steer. Offsetting the picture requires the observer to focus attention on a set of numbers in a small box that is away from the picture when using an EBL (electronic bearing line). A mechanical cursor becomes useless when using the offset center because the outer scale cannot be utilized.
- If necessary, switch the range scale to the 1½-mile range to look ahead.
- On Alaska Marine Highway System vessels, the *Relative Stabilized North Up presentation* is good. This orientation stabilizes the picture while instantly showing the trails of vessels that are under way, making it easy to distinguish aids to navigation from moving vessels. North is always up, and the heading flash moves to indicate the true heading. Some prefer the *Relative Unstabilized Ship's Head Up presentation*. This presentation gives the view one actually sees from the wheelhouse windows, but the picture and targets move when the course changes. In this orientation, the ship's heading is up all the time and does not move. These are individual preferences.

Maxims

- Have the most competent helmsman steer through Peril Strait, especially through Sergius and Whitestone Narrows.

- Adjust and tune radars for maximum picture clarity with rain and sea clutter turned down to a minimum, if not off entirely.
- A lookout should be in place on the bow. Have an anchor ready for immediate release.
- Engines should be on standby and ready for immediate maneuver.
- Instruct mates to speak out immediately if something does not look correct.
- Teamwork is necessary in fog or heavy snow. One mate should listen to the conning orders, watching the radars in case of error. Another mate should verify that conning orders are carried out, respond to the VHF radio, and fill in the logbook.
- Filling in a logbook is secondary to the safe navigation of the vessel.
- Be vigilant for unlighted skiffs traveling at high speed at night.
- Have a searchlight with a strong beam of light ready for use.
- Turn on either a fathometer or recording fathometer.
- The VHF radios should monitor channels 13 and 16. Make sure the squelch is turned to its proper setting to minimize static noise.
- When lined up on a range, the course may be compared with the actual range direction. The difference is a vessel's compass error. Whitestone Narrows is an excellent place to check for compass error.
- On vessels equipped with automatic radar plotting aids (ARPA), a mate should be employed to plot any vessel targets.
- Peril Strait can be a challenge even in the best of circumstances.

Limitations

- On Alaska Marine Highway System vessels, the in-house rule is to enter Sergius Narrows no more than half an hour either side of the time of slack water, preferably as close to slack water as possible. The depth is not an issue; the strength of the current is the problem.
  - › In Whitestone Narrows, depth and current are usually not a problem for most vessels. However, on the lower tides below datum, bottom suction or squatting may occur, especially near Whitestone Narrows Lighted Buoy 17 at the northern end. The M/V *Kennicott* uses a +2.0 foot holdover for transiting Whitestone Narrows. Drawing only 13.5 feet of water, the smaller M/V *LeConte* and *Aurora* transit Whitestone Narrows at low water, but slowly.
- Entering Peril Strait in the fog is at the discretion of the master. When initiating a turn in clear visibility, it is valuable to memorize distances off points of land or objects that are abeam. This serves as a safeguard in case of reduced visibility.
- A vessel can experience bank cushion, bank suction, and squatting on lower tides, especially at Whitestone Narrows and Middle Shoal in Olga Strait. The vessel should slow down, but only enough to reduce the above conditions while retaining firm control.
- Using buoys for reference, headings, and course changes is always risky, as they may drift out of position due to wind and current.

Currents

- From *US Coast Pilot 8*, we read, "The flood current from Salisbury Sound sets northeast through Sergius Narrows and Adams Channel and meets the flood from Chatham Strait in the broad part of Peril Strait between Povorotni Island and Otstoia Island; the ebb current sets in the opposite direction. In Peril Strait, the strongest currents are in Sergius Narrows, where the velocity is 5.9 knots on the flood and 5.5 knots on the ebb. For other places in the strait, the velocity of the current is between 1.4 and 2.5 knots."[77] However, greater current velocities are possible in conditions of deep low-pressure weather systems, strong winds, and large tide ranges.

- In Neva Strait, the currents flow northward on the ebb current and southward on the flood current with an average speed of 1.4 knots. The currents meet and separate in the basin of Krestof Sound to the southwest of Whitestone Narrows. The flood flows north from Sitka Sound through Hayward Strait,

77 *United States Coast Pilot 8*, 208.

Sergius Narrows Buoy 8 being pulled underwater on a strong ebb current in Sergius Narrows as observed on the FVF *Fairweather*. PHOTO COURTESY OF CAPTAIN WAYNE CARNES.

south from Neva Strait, and northwest through Olga Strait to Krestof Sound. On the ebb, the waters flow from Krestof Sound south into Sitka Sound through Hayward Strait, north to Salisbury Sound through Neva Strait, and southeast through Olga Strait.

- In Olga Strait, the flood current flows northwestward, and the ebb current flows southeastward to and from Krestof Sound. At Creek Point, the current's velocity is 1.6 knots on the flood and 1.2 knots on the ebb.
- Transits are timed to be at Sergius Narrows within a half-hour of either high or low water slack. By state ferry, it is approximately 105 minutes from the ferry terminal at Sitka to Sergius Narrows and 60 minutes from Broad Island to Sergius Narrows. All arrivals and departures from Sitka revolve around the time of slack water at Sergius Narrows.

Charts and Publications

- *US Coast Pilot 8* offers a good description of Peril Strait, Sergius Narrows, Neva Strait, Whitestone Narrows, and Olga Strait. It is wise to study it in detail.
- Keep the *Coast Pilot*, charts, and *Light List* corrected up to the most recent edition of the *Local Notices to Mariners*. Peril Strait is depicted on NOAA Nautical Charts 17338, 17323, and 17324. Use only the latest edition.
- Pay particular attention to *CG 169—The Nautical Rules of the Road*: Rule 9, Narrow Channels; Rule 13, Overtaking; Rule 19, Conduct of Vessels in Restricted Visibility; and Rule 35, Sound Signals in Restricted Visibility.

General Interest

- The distance from Morris Reef Lighted Buoy 35 to the Alaska State Ferry Terminal at Peril Strait is 59.5 nautical miles.
- There are 36 course changes along the route.

- There are 50 aids to navigation for the main channel, excluding any dock lights.

Channel Depths

- A federal project depth is the design dredging depth of a channel. The federal project depth provides for the several dredged sections at Sergius Narrows and Whitestone Narrows of 24 feet. The federal project also provides for a channel width of 450 feet in Sergius Narrows and 300 feet in Whitestone Narrows.
- Recent surveys by the Army Corps of Engineers indicate a least depth of 22.5 feet midchannel near Whitestone Narrows Lighted Buoy 17 and a least depth of 11 feet on the edge of the channel immediately south of Whitestone Narrows Light 14.
- The controlling depth is the least depth in the channel; it is the result of silting and filling in over time. For controlling depths, consult regularly with *Local Notices to Mariners.*
- Extreme high barometric pressure can also cause tides to be unpredictably lower than is tabulated.
- Several times a year, exceptionally large spring tides occur, and the water level may fall as much as three feet below the chart datum.

Weather

- *Coast Pilot 8* states: "Salisbury Sound is open to prevailing wind and sea from the Gulf of Alaska, whereas Peril Strait is sheltered somewhat by Chichagof Island. In the sound, SW swells frequently roll in and break along the N shore, sometimes reaching Baranof Island. Winds often draw through Salisbury Sound and into Peril Strait, which, because of its orientation, is susceptible to both strong southeasterlies and northerlies. These winds are most likely from October through February. Heavy fog sometimes moves into the sound but frequently disappears at the mouths of Fish Bay and Neva Strait. Occasionally, the fog reaches Peril Strait as far as Sergius Narrows and sometimes fills the strait north of the narrows."[78]

Russian Place Name Lexicon

Otstoia	distant
Opasni	dangerous
Elovoi	spruce island
Krugloi	round
Povorotni	turnabout
Pogibshi	perilous
Siroi	wet
Liesnoi	wooded
Sergius	a Russian male first name
Prolewy	an English corruption of the Russian word *proliv,* meaning *strait*
Suloia	ripple
Struya	ripples caused by tidal currents
Kakul	derived from the word *kekur,* a Russian derivation of a Native word meaning "a high, isolated rock or rocky inlet"
Goloi	bare
Kalinin	a Russian surname
Sinitsin	a Russian surname
Sukoi	dry
Partofshikof	a Russian surname
Neva	name of an early Russian American Company ship
Olga	a Russian female first name. Olga Strait is named for the SV *Olga,* the first ship built in Alaska at

78 *United States Coast Pilot 8,* 207.

	Resurrection Bay (Seward).[79] The strait's original name was Proliv Krestovskoy, meaning cross strait.
Krestof	cross harbor
Starrigavan	from the Russian compound word *starri gavan*, meaning *old harbor*. The first Russian settlement in Southeastern Alaska was founded on the shores of this bay in 1799. The bay acquired its name in 1802, after the settlement in 1802 was relocated to present-day Sitka.
Vitskari	a Russian word meaning Captain Witz's chastisement
Makhnati (*mokhnatyy*)	rough or rugged
Kulichkof	snipe
Bieli	white[80]

Commercial and Sport Fishing

- Winter salmon troll*:* Runs from October 1 to mid-April. Trollers can be found anywhere but seem most prevalent at Kakul Narrows and Salisbury Sound.
- Summer salmon troll*:* Runs April 15–September 30. These vessels are numerous, especially between Cape Edgecumbe and Vitskari Rock in Sitka Sound.
- Summer salmon seine fishery*:* Established by emergency order and usually begins on a Sunday. Heavy concentrations can occur between Sergius Narrows and Entrance Island.
- Commercial pot shrimp fishing*:* Runs from October 1 to the end of February. Season is closed from March to mid-May to protect the fishery during the egg hatch and release period.

79 Roppel, unpublished notes.

80 Orth, *Dictionary of Alaska Place Names*.

If some quotas are not filled, the season opens again after mid-May.

- Red king crab*:* Runs from November 1 to the end of January, depending on abundance, at Rodman Bay, Deadman Reach, and Ushk Bay.
- Brown king crab*:* Runs on the waters of Peril Strait to Neva Point from mid-February until closed by emergency order.
- Dungeness crab*:* Runs mostly on the waters of Sitka Sound from October 1 to the end of February. There can also be a June 15–August 15 summer fishery.
- Tanner crab*:* Harvested from mid-February to May 1.
- Abalone*:* Dive fishery runs from October 1 through mid-May.
- Sea cucumber fishery: Dive fishery runs from October 1 to the end of March and mostly occurs on the waters of Sitka Sound.
- Red sea urchin fishery: Dive fishery runs from October 1 to the end of September.
- Herring winter food and bait fishery: Established by emergency order only. Runs from October 1 to the end of February in the Sitka Sound and Salisbury Sound areas.
- Herring spawn on kelp fishery: Runs from mid-March to the end of April at Hoonah Sound.
- Sitka herring sac roe seine fishery: This fishery has perhaps the greatest effect on Alaska Marine Highway operations, often taking place directly off the Alaska State Ferry Terminal in Sitka. A vessel will nearly be pinned in by seine nets and seining vessels if the fishery opens while the boat is moored to the dock. This fishery opens in March or April, depending on the time of the spawn.
- Ground fish fisheries: These are many and varied. They occur mostly offshore in the eastern Gulf of Alaska. These fisheries

include lingcod, sole, pollock, sablefish, demersal rockfish, flounder, and halibut. Sitka has a large fleet of groundfishers.

Range Bearings

- Whitestone Narrows Range: 345 degrees true northbound, 165 degrees true southbound.

Hydrographic Surveys

- Detailed hydrographic surveys of Sergius Narrows and Whitestone Narrows can be obtained from the Army Corps of Engineers by writing to:

  Alaska District Office
  Army Corps of Engineers
  Bldg. 21-700
  Elmendorf Air Force Base
  Box 898
  Anchorage, AK 99506-0898

General Precautions

- It is usually easier to start a turn early and check the vessel's swing than to turn so late that the ship cannot respond quickly enough.
- While executing a turn, when and how much rudder to use depends on the strength and direction of the current and whether a ship is traveling against (stemming) or with the current.
- Be aware of potential wake damage, especially while passing Dog Point when inbound. With respect to other areas and situations, the current velocity, water depth, and the handling characteristics of the vessel determine the maximum speed that the ship can safely travel.

- When overtaking another vessel in the narrows, remember that the vessel being overtaken has the right of way. If possible, reduce speed in time to overtake the other vessel at a safe location. If this is not practicable, try to make meeting arrangements via the VHF radio to overtake where the channel widens.
- In the summer, expect recreational boating traffic in the form of both yachts and sport charter vessels. Sometimes the operators of these vessels do not pay attention to the presence of larger vessels.
- When meeting another vessel in the narrows, try whenever possible to arrange for one vessel to wait outside the narrows until the other vessel clears. If this is not practicable, arrange on VHF radio to meet at a wide portion of the channel, adjusting the speed in accordance with that of the other vessel in order to meet at a safe location. Frequent communication with the meeting vessel for updates on its position is essential.
- If a vessel that is ahead offers to pull aside, do not discourage it from doing so. It is always best to get around the vessel ahead and have it fall in behind at the earliest opportunity.
- Exercise common sense and good judgment. A ship's pilot should never feel pressured into taking an unnecessary risk.
- Above all, maintain concentration. Keep pilothouse chatter to a minimum.

NOAA Nautical Chart 17323: Salisbury Sound, Peril Strait, and Hoonah Sound

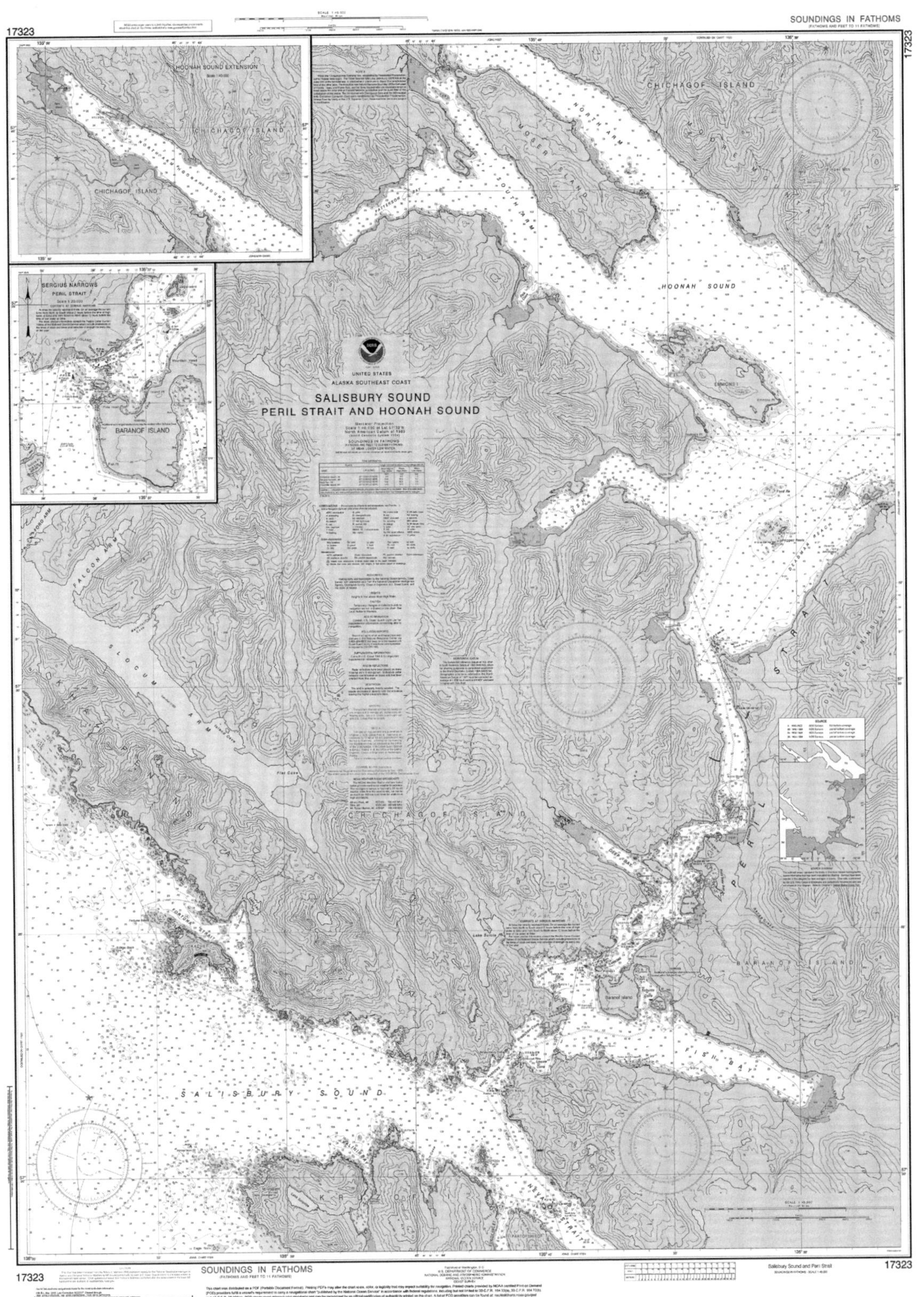

NOAA Nautical Chart 17324: Sitka Sound to Salisbury Sound Inside Passage

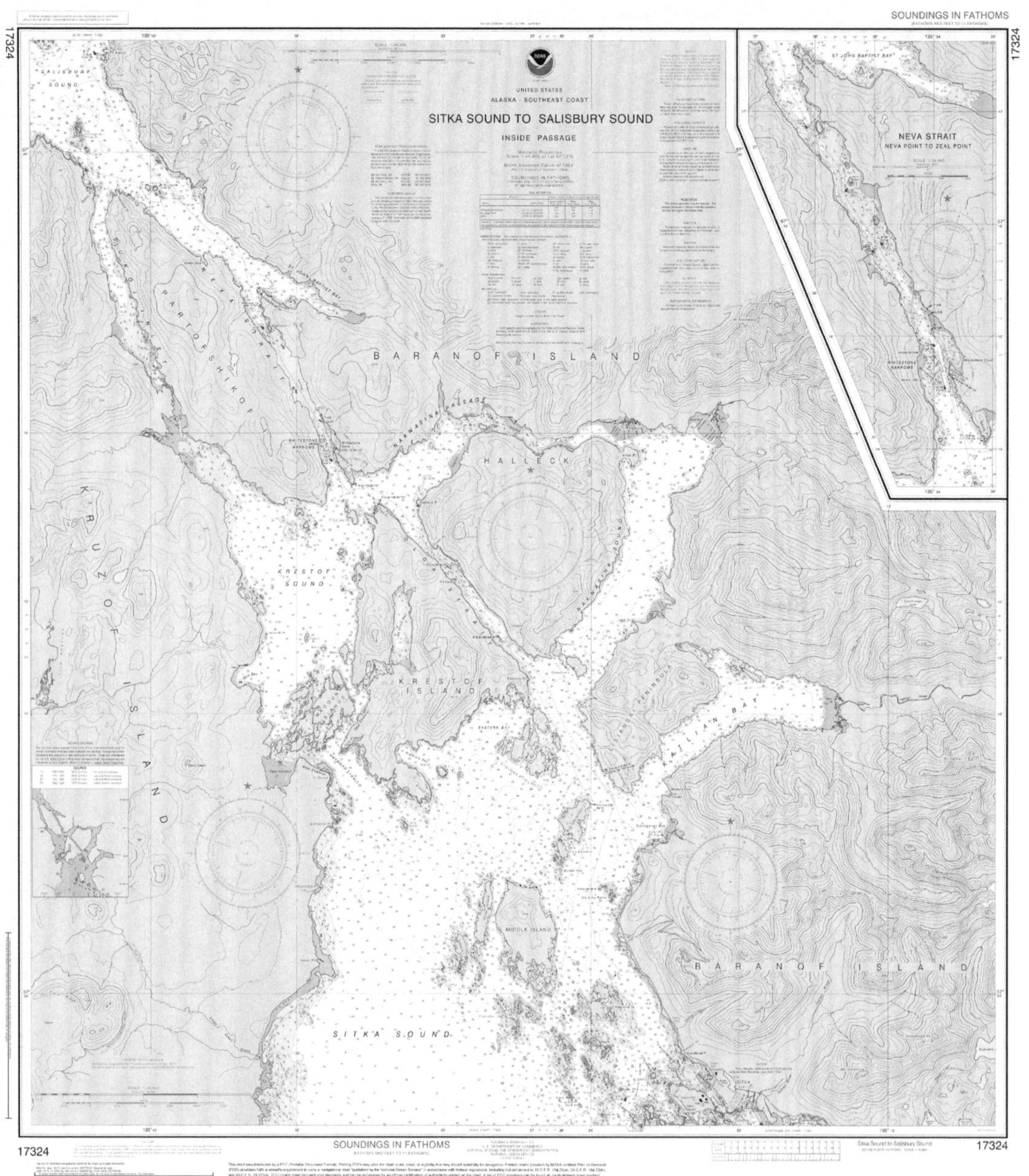

NOAA Nautical Chart 17326: Crawfish Inlet to Sitka

Peril Strait Course Card

Sitka Inbound

Morris Reef	265	Channel Rocks	217
McClellan Rock	288	Kakul Rock	171
F. Lindenberg Hd.	309	Scraggy Island	136
Pos.Broad Is.	265	Kane Island	136
Elovoi Island	194	Entrance Island	158
Hoggatt Reef	234	Highwater Is	146
Povorotni Is	158	Dirty Water Pt.	167
Lt. #22	174	Wyville Reef	147
Nixon Shoal	165	Whitestone Pt.	165
Big Rose Is.	260	Whitestone Rk	153
Yellow Pt	215	Neva Point	090
Middle Pt	180	Olga Point	145
Big Island	214	Creek Point	125
Pt. Siroi	224	Middle Shoal	144
Lesnoi Shoal	254	Olga Strait Pos	140
Point Sinbad	180	Lt. #5	137
Suloia Point	214	Eastern Point	153
Struya Point	256	Big Gavanski	140

Peril Strait Course Card

Sitka Outbound

Depart AMHS	312	Channel Rocks	076
Big Gavanski	333	Struya Point	032
Eastern Point	317	Suloia Point	348
Lt. #5	320	Point Sinbad	070
Olga Strait Pos	325	Lesnoi Shoal	045
Middle Shoal	305	Pt. Siroi	034
Creek Point	325	Big Island	000
Olga Point	270	Middle Pt.	034
Neva Point	333	Yellow Pt.	077
Whitestone Pos	345	Big Rose Is.	345
Whitestone Pt.	328	Nixon Shoal	354
Wyville Reef	345	Lt. #22	338
Dirty Water Pt.	326	Povorotni Is	054
Highwater Is	338	Hoggatt Reef	014
Entrance Island	316	Elovoi Island	085
Kane Island	316	Broad Is	129
Scraggy Island	352	F. Lindenberg Hd.	108
Kakul Rock	037	McClellan Rock	085

Distance Chart

Morris Reef Lighted Buoy to the Alaska State Ferry Terminal at Sitka

	Morris Reef Lighted Buoy	Fairway Island Light	McClellan Rock	False Lindenberg Head	Broad Island First	Broad Island Second	Krugloi Island	Hoggatt Reef	Povorotni Island	Light # 22	Big Rose Island	Middle Point	Liesnoi Shoal	Sergius Narrows Light	Suloia Point	Channel Rocks	Kane Island	Entrance Island	Whitestone Point	Neva Point	Middle Shoal	Eastern Point	Lisianski Point
Fairway Island Light	2.2																						
McClellan Rock	7.2	5.0																					
False Lindenberg Head	9.4	7.4	2.4																				
Broad Island First	21.1	18.9	13.9	11.5																			
Broad Island Second	21.8	19.6	14.6	12.2	0.7																		
Krugloi Island	24.4	22.2	17.2	14.8	3.3	2.6																	
Hoggatt Reef	26.2	24.0	19.0	16.6	5.1	4.4	1.8																
Povorotni Island	29.0	26.8	21.8	19.4	7.9	7.2	4.6	2.8															
Light # 22	30.7	28.5	23.5	21.1	9.6	8.9	6.3	4.5	1.7														
Big Rose Island	33.0	30.8	25.8	23.4	11.9	11.2	8.6	6.8	4.0	2.3													
Middle Point	34.7	32.5	27.5	25.1	13.6	12.9	10.3	8.5	5.7	4.0	1.7												
Liesnoi Shoal	36.7	34.5	29.5	27.1	15.6	14.9	12.3	10.5	7.7	6.0	3.7	2.0											
Sergius Narrows Light	37.5	35.3	30.3	27.9	16.4	15.7	13.1	11.3	8.5	6.8	4.5	2.8	0.8										
Suloia Point	38.9	36.7	31.7	29.3	17.8	17.1	14.5	12.7	9.9	8.2	5.9	4.2	2.2	1.4									
Channel Rocks	40.6	38.4	33.4	31.0	19.5	18.8	16.2	14.4	11.6	9.9	7.6	5.9	3.9	3.1	1.7								
Kane Island	44.4	42.2	37.2	34.8	23.3	22.6	20.0	18.2	15.4	13.7	11.4	9.7	7.7	6.9	5.5	3.8							
Entrance Island	47.1	44.9	39.9	37.5	26.0	25.3	22.7	20.9	18.1	16.4	14.1	12.4	10.4	9.6	8.2	6.5	1.7						
Whitestone Point	50.0	47.8	42.8	40.4	28.9	28.2	26.5	23.8	21.0	19.3	17.0	15.3	13.3	12.5	11.1	9.4	5.6	2.9					
Neva Point	50.8	48.6	43.6	41.2	29.7	29.0	27.3	24.6	21.8	20.1	17.8	16.1	14.1	13.3	11.9	10.2	6.4	3.7	0.8				
Middle Shoal	53.3	51.1	46.1	43.7	32.2	31.5	28.9	27.1	24.3	22.6	20.3	18.6	16.6	15.8	14.4	12.7	8.9	6.2	3.3	2.5			
Eastern Point	55.8	53.6	48.6	46.2	34.7	34.0	31.4	29.6	26.8	25.1	22.8	21.1	19.1	18.3	16.9	15.2	11.4	8.7	5.8	5.0	2.5		
Lisianski Point	57.8	55.7	50.7	48.3	36.8	36.1	33.5	31.7	28.9	27.2	24.9	23.2	21.2	20.4	19.0	17.3	13.5	10.8	7.9	7.1	4.6	2.1	
Dock Sitka	59.5	***57.3***	52.3	49.9	38.4	37.7	35.1	33.3	30.5	28.8	26.5	24.8	22.8	22.0	20.6	18.9	15.1	12.4	9.5	8.7	6.2	3.7	1.6

Halfway point between Morris Reef and the Alaska State Ferry Terminal at Sitka

Halfway point between Povorotni Island and the Alaska State Ferry Terminal at Sitka

Total distance between Morris Reef and the Alaska State Ferry Terminal at Sitka

Peril Strait

Inbound to Sitka

Inbound to Sitka

When approaching the eastern entrance of Peril Strait in Chatham Strait from the north, take care to avoid the extensive Morris Reef complex of ledges and submerged rocks southeast of Point Hayes. A line from Morris Reef Lighted Buoy 35 to the tangent of Peninsular Point passes along the eastern edge of Morris Reef, making a good danger bearing. It is advisable to stay well away from this line of danger. Most of the foul ground lies to the west of the line, but some is also just east of it.

When southbound in Chatham Strait, shape the course to pass 1.40 NM off Peninsular Point. From Peninsular Point, maintain a course of 187 degrees true, heading tangent to Point Lull on Catherine Island and passing 0.50 NM off the Morris Reef Lighted Buoy 35. Round the buoy slowly to starboard, maintaining a distance of 0.50 NM off the buoy. Bear in mind that using a floating aid to navigation is risky business, as the buoy may shift position.

Use a radar cursor or the radar's parallel indexing capability to set up the next course of 265 degrees to pass 0.50 NM north of Fairway Island Light 32 and 0.70 NM south of the Point Craven Light as a safety measure. This will ensure that a vessel maintains a safe distance off Morris Reef regardless of the buoy's position. Once steadied on course 265 degrees true to pass 0.50 NM north of Fairway Island Light 32, a vessel has safely made its entrance into Peril Strait. Maintain course 265 degrees true to pass 0.50 NM south of McClellan Rock Light, just off Lindenberg Head.

When approaching the eastern entrance of Peril Strait in Chatham Strait from the south, shape the course to pass 1.30 NM off Point Thatcher. The northward heading in Chatham Strait is usually 349 degrees true with the Morris Reef Lighted Buoy 35 dead ahead. This heading is tangent to Peninsular Point.

Once abeam of Point Thatcher, change course to the port and steady up on course 325 degrees true. This course heads on an unnamed peninsular point separating Florence Bay from Sitkoh Bay, with the Point Craven Light to the left of this heading. This unnamed point makes a good radar mark on which to steer. The heading will keep a vessel 0.80 NM to the east of Midway Reef, a small reef that must be kept in mind when approaching the Peril Strait entrance from the south.

Again, by using the radar cursor or parallel indexing, set up the next course of 265 degrees true to pass 0.50 NM north of Fairway Island Light 32 and 0.70 NM south of the Point Craven Light. Set the radar VRM (variable range ring) to 1.25 NM. When Point Craven touches this ring, it is time to change course.

When the time is right, change the course to the port and steady up on 265 degrees true, passing 0.50 NM north of Fairway Island Light 32 and 0.50 NM south of McClellan Rock Light, just off Lindenberg Head.

Once entrance into Peril Strait has been made, the waters for the next 19.6 miles from Fairway Island to Broad Island are deep and wide.

1. **McClellan Rock Light to False Lindenberg Head:** Maintain a distance of 0.50 NM off McClellan Rock Light and come to starboard to course 288 degrees true to pass 0.70 NM south of False Lindenberg Head. This heading falls on the tip of land north of the bight northwest of Saook Point, midway between Saook Point and Point Benham. If it is desired to be farther from the starboard beach, use the left-hand tangent of the bight.

2. **False Lindenberg Head to Broad Island:** This course is the longest reach in Peril Strait at 12.2 NM. Maintain a distance of 0.70

NM off False Lindenberg Head and come to starboard to course 310 degrees true. Broad Island is then dead ahead. Broad Island is both a good visual mark and a good radar mark. Maintain a distance of 0.80 NM off the Point Benham Light and a distance of 0.80 NM off Peschani Point.

As the vessel approaches Broad Island, set the radar VRM to 0.75 NM to prepare for the next course change. When the 0.75 VRM ring touches Broad Island ahead, turn to port and come to course 265 degrees true. A visual cue to determine when to change course at Broad Island is the Cozian Reef Light 3 immediately east of Otstoia Island. When the Cozian Reef Light 3 passes two-thirds the distance in front of Otstoia Island in the background, it is time to change the course to 265 degrees true.

Alternative Route: When abeam and 0.80 NM off the conspicuous unnamed point northwest of Peschani Point, change course to port and steady up on 295 degrees true. This heading will be on the right tangent of hat-shaped Emmons Island in Hoonah Sound. When abeam of Broad Island Light on the starboard side, change the course to 265 degrees true, heading on the south tangent of Ushk Point ahead on the north side of the entrance of Ushk Bay.

3. **Broad Island to Elovoi Island:** The heading of 265 degrees true should be tangent to Ushk Point on the north side of the entrance of Ushk Bay. Pass 0.55 NM to the north of Elovoi Island Light 26. To the starboard is the very beautiful Hoonah Sound, a good place to await the tide if early for a slack water passage of Sergius Narrows.

   Note: For a vessel traveling at 15–16 knots, it is one hour from Broad Island to Sergius Narrows. It is 30 minutes from Broad Island to Povorotni Island.

4. **Elovoi Island Light 26 to Hoggatt Reef Light 25:** This is a gradual turn to port. When making this turn, look to a lineup between the Povorotni Island Light and Hoggatt Reef Light 25. You do not want to pass to the west beyond this line before starting the turn. This

is done to avoid getting too close to Ford Rock. Make the turn to pass 0.55 NM off Elovoi Island the second time and 0.45 NM off the southwest end of Krugloi Island. Come to course 192 degrees true to pass 0.55 NM east of Hoggatt Island. Visually, the vessel should be heading on the notch on the ridgeline ahead.

Note: Hoggatt Island is a very low and flat island that makes a poor radar target. Hoggatt Reef Light 25, however, does make a radar target. This light is critical to make the next turn to starboard for Povorotni Island.

Note: When running late for the tide at Sergius Narrows, a good place to anchor is at Favorite Anchorage in Deadman Reach to await the next slack water at Sergius Narrows, 1.20 NM southwest of Otstoia Island and 0.20 NM from shore in 17 fathoms. Anchorage can be made in several places along the Baranof Island shoreline, including Pogibshi Anchorage at Goose Cove in 20 fathoms. Deadman Reach is subject to williwaw wind conditions in the winter months when any gale-force winds blow from the southwest around to the south and southeast.

Note: Hoggatt Island and Deadman Reach is the place to give a Securité call on high power for transiting Peril Strait and Sergius Narrows when inbound.

Deadman Reach

5. **Hoggatt Reef Light 25 to Povorotni Island Light:** Change the course to starboard when Hoggatt Reef Light 25 is slightly forward of the starboard beam. Use a moderate amount of rudder and come to course 234 degrees true. Do not wait too long to start this turn.

   Look to the ridgeline directly behind and above Povorotni Island. There is a visible notch in the timber that navigators have used for many years. The heading of 234 degrees should be on this notch or close to it. This natural feature is called Dagle's Notch, named for Captain Tillman Dagle, master and pilot with the Alaska Steamship Company and the Alaska Marine Highway System. This heading is tangent to a small point opposite Povorotni Island near the south entrance point to Poison Cove. Pass 0.25 NM north of Povorotni Island Light.

Note: At Povorotni Island, Peril Strait becomes very narrow. It is approximately 30 minutes to Sergius Narrows.

6. **Povorotni Island Light to Flat Point Light 22:** Changing course at Povorotni Island is generally known as a beam turn, keeping the light abeam all the way around. Begin this turn when Big Rose Island Light 21 opens into view. Keep the light in sight to keep from getting too far to the right. Change course to port with a moderate amount of rudder to pass midway between Povorotni Island and the Chichagof Island shore. Try to stay midchannel. Steady up on course 158 degrees true, with Flat Point Light 22 showing ahead on the port side. Steer on the knoll ahead.

   Note: When steadied up on a course of 158 degrees true, the Big Rose Island Light 21 should be in range with the Chichagof Island shore. This puts a ship midchannel. Keep well clear of the shoals extending from Chichagof Island. It is safer to be east of the track than to be west of it.

7. **Flat Point Light 22 to Nixon Shoal:** When Flat Point Light 22 is well forward of the port beam, come to starboard and steady up on course 174 degrees true. This course should be heading on the Big Rose Island Light 21, the east or left tangent of Big Rose Island.

8. **Nixon Shoal to Big Rose Island Light 21:** Nixon Shoal is a low, grass-covered gravel bar on the port side along the Baranof Island shoreline. Come to port when Nixon Shoal is slightly forward of the port beam and steady up on course 165 degrees true. Another method is to set the VRM to 0.55 NM and change course when the VRM ring touches Little Rose Island ahead. The ship should be midchannel between Big Rose Island and the Baranof Island shore. Head on the creek; the notch is evident on the radar. The

unnamed east point on the Chichagof Island shore should be astern. Be aware that during periods of high water, Nixon Shoal is submerged and easy to miss by running past the course change point.

Note: The channel east of Big Rose Island is the Adams Channel. The channel to the west is the Rose Channel. Smaller vessels hoping to avoid traffic can use the Rose Channel.

Note: Avoid meeting other vessels before committing to the turn at Big Rose Island.

Adams Channel

9. **Big Rose Island Light 21 to Yellow Point Light 16:** This is a large, sweeping course change. Start swinging to starboard using a moderate amount of rudder before coming abeam of Big Rose Island Light 21. Gauge the turn to remain midchannel, rounding Rose Island Rock Light 19 close to starboard. As a general rule, be 0.08 NM off Rose Island Rock Light 19. Avoid the shallow gravel flats off the mouth of Range Creek along the Baranof Island shore when making this turn. Do not make a lazy turn, as the vessel may get too close to these shallow flats. Steady up on course 260 degrees true. This heading will be on the south tangent of Arthur Island dead ahead.

10. **Yellow Point Light 16 to Middle Point Light 14:** Come to port with Yellow Point Light 16 forward of the port beam with a moderate amount of rudder. Steady up on course 214 degrees true to be heading inside the small notch on the east end of Big Island. Be aware of the covered 12-foot shoal area southeast of Arthur Island nearly one-third the distance across the channel.

11. **Middle Point Light 14 to the little islet just off Big Island:** With Middle Point Light 14 three points forward of the port beam, come to port with a moderate amount of rudder and steady up on course 180 degrees true. This heading will be on the west

tangent of Bear Bay Island. Be aware of the 19-foot shoal off the east side of the little islet just off Big Island.

12. **Little islet just off Big Island to Point Siroi Light 12:** When abeam of the little islet off Big Island, come to starboard using a moderate amount of rudder and steady up on course 214 degrees true to pass west of the Point Siroi Light. Other lineups to start this turn include when this islet closes with Liesnoi Island, or when the Deep Bay Entrance Daybeacon 1 atop Grasstop Rock is between Big Island and the little islet off Big Island. This course heading will be on the west tangent of Mountain Head.

    Note: When approaching Point Siroi, Suloia Point Light 5 and Pinta Head make a natural range with Liesnoi Shoal Lighted Buoy 11 marking a shoal covered by eight feet of water. This gives a good indication as to whether or not Liesnoi Shoal Buoy 11 is on station.

13. **Point Siroi Light 12 to Liesnoi Shoal Lighted Buoy 11:** When abeam of Point Siroi, or slightly past abeam, come to starboard and steady up on course 222 degrees true. Pass midchannel between Liesnoi Shoal Lighted Buoy 11 and Mountain Head, staying about 0.10 NM off the Mountain Head shore.

    Note: From Point Siroi Light 12, it is five minutes to Sergius Narrows.

Sergius Narrows

14. **Liesnoi Shoal Lighted Buoy 11 to West Francis Rock Lighted Buoy 6–Sergius Narrows:** Come to the starboard when the Liesnoi Shoal Lighted Buoy 11 is two or more points forward of the starboard beam or when this buoy and the Sergius Point Light 9 line up in range with one another. Change course with a moderate amount of rudder and steady up on a course of 252 degrees true. Focus sharply on Sergius Narrows ahead. Wayanda Ledge Buoy

10 and Sergius Narrows Buoy 8 are nearly in range. West Francis Rock Lighted Buoy 6 is to the left of this lineup.

Start the transit of Sergius Narrows on course 252 degrees true, heading nearly on Sergius Point Light 9. Adjust the course as necessary to transit Sergius Narrows between Sergius Point Light 9 and Wayanda Ledge Buoy 10. Most navigators will favor the Wayanda Ledge side of the channel instead of the Sergius Point side. Be aware of the submerged rock off Shoal Point.

Note: Slow down a little when making a transit of Sergius Narrows. The old-timers always recommended keeping some reserve power in your back pocket in case of need.

Sergius Narrows Buoy 8 in strong current as observed onboard the FVF *Fairweather*. PHOTO COURTESY OF CAPTAIN WAYNE CARNES.

Note: If any flood current is present, expect turbulent water and a set to the right. Upwelling and swirls occur between Wayanda Reef Buoy 10 and Liesnoi Shoal Lighted Buoy 11 on flood currents.

If any ebb current is present, it generally flows with the axis of the channel. Upwelling and swirls occur north of West Francis Rock Lighted Buoy 6 to Point Sinbad on ebb currents.

15. **West Francis Lighted Buoy 6 to Suloia Point Light 5:** Passing through Sergius Narrows, stay on course to give the West Francis

Wayanda Ledge Buoy 10 and Sergius Narrows Buoy 8 in strong current as observed onboard the FVF *Fairweather*. PHOTO COURTESY OF CAPTAIN WAYNE CARNES.

Rock Lighted Buoy 6 a wide berth to avoid the foul ground in the West Francis Rock area. When abeam of the buoy, come around to port with a moderate amount of rudder and steady up on course 180 degrees true. Pass to be at least 0.15 NM east of Suloia Point Light 5.

16. **Suloia Point Light 5 to Struya Point:** When Suloia Point Light 5 is abaft the beam, or when Channel Rocks Light 4 comes into view, change course to the starboard with a moderate amount of rudder and steady up on course 215 degrees true. This heading should be on the west tangent of Range Point. Prepare for the next course change by observing the high top of Struya Point or the old landslide area on the side of Struya Point.

17. **Struya Point to Channel Rocks Light 4:** When abeam of the old landslide or the very top of Struya Point hill, come to starboard and steady up on course 256 degrees true. This course should be heading into Salmonberry Cove just to the north of Brad Rock Light 3 or on the "Foul" point south tangent on the chart.

    Note: The skyline of Struya Point is visible at nighttime. This is why the very top of Struya Point hill makes a good mark for making this course change to 256 degrees true.

    Note: When near Struya Point, Suloia Point, and Fish Bay, a navigator must be aware of the unmarked and dangerous Haley Rocks, covered with four feet of water. Note also the bare rock immediately northwest of Range Point.

Kakul Narrows

18. **Channel Rocks Light 4 to Kakul Rock Lighted Buoy 2–Kakul Narrows:** When on a course of 256 degrees true, water can be seen between the Channel Rocks Light 4 and the Baranof Island shoreline. Come to the port with a healthy amount of rudder when the view of Channel Rock Light 4 closes or touches with the Baranof Island shoreline. Steady up on course 217 degrees true, passing

Brad Rock Light 3 on the starboard side. Be cautious of turning too fast and steering past the new course.

You can also set the radar's EBL to a course of 217 degrees true. When this line is tangent to the Point Kakul shoreline, begin the course change. Another method is to set the radar's VRM to 0.30 NM. When the ring touches the unnamed point ahead denoted on the chart by "Foul," begin the course change.

Note: Another visual indicator occurs when the Kakul Rock Lighted Buoy 2 comes into view, providing it is on station.

Salisbury Sound

19. Kakul Rock Lighted Buoy 2 to Scraggy Island: When Round Island is slightly forward of the beam on the starboard side, come to port and steady up on course 172 degrees true. This turn may also be started when the view of Kakul Rock Lighted Buoy 2 closes with the land on the port side. The heading of 172 degrees true should be on the west tangent of Partofshikof Island ahead at the entrance of Sukoi Inlet. Set the radar VRM to 0.60 NM.

Note: A good swell from the Gulf of Alaska can roll well into Salisbury Sound; however, the exposure to the swell is of short duration.

Note: Fog can move into Peril Strait and Neva Strait from Salisbury Sound.

Neva Strait

20. Scraggy Island to Entrance Island: When the 0.60 NM VRM ring touches Scraggy Island off the starboard bow, come to port and steady up on course 136 degrees true. Another method to gauge this turn is to come abeam on the port side of the bight or sharp indentation in the shoreline 0.70 NM south of Point Kakul. On the starboard side, come abeam of the unnamed channel separating Sinitsin Island from Kruzof Island.

When on course 136 degrees true, pass 0.10–0.12 NM off the Kane Island Light 25 on the starboard side. Be mindful of the rocks on the port side off the Baranof Island shore. Once past the Kane Islands, set the VRM once again to 0.60 NM. The heading of 136 degrees true should be on the east tangent of Entrance Island and Zeal Point ahead.

Note: The area between Kane Islands and Entrance Island is a good location to await traffic to clear before entering Neva Strait at Highwater Island and Whitestone Narrows.

Note: It is approximately 20 minutes from Kane Island to Whitestone Narrows and 70 minutes to the Alaska State Ferry Terminal.

21. Entrance Island Light 24 to Highwater Island Lighted Buoy 23: When the 0.60 NM VRM ring touches Entrance Island, come to starboard and steady up on course 158 degrees true heading on the Highwater Island Lighted Buoy 23 or keeping the buoy slightly on the starboard side. Be aware of the covered 14-foot rock that is about 100 yards off the Partofshikoff Island shore on the starboard side opposite from Entrance Island. This rock shows kelp growth in the summer months, but not in the winter months.

On the port side, be aware of the rock outcropping approximately 800 yards northwest of Highwater Island along the shoreline. Visually, this course change can be made when Highwater Island closes with the far point of Partofshikof Island in the distance.

Note: After making the course change at Entrance Island, the vessel should reduce speed to half ahead or to a no-wake speed. The waters ahead become very shallow and narrow.

Note: In order to mark course change locations where there were no official aids to navigation, Captain Bill Mitchell of the Alaska Marine Highway System placed reflector boards at strategic positions in Neva and Olga Straits. They are known as Mitchell Markers.

When nearing the Entrance Island course change on a heading of 136 degrees true, the starboard Partofshikof Island shoreline is uneven with several small indentations southeast of Gilmer Cove. In the last of these shore indentations, just north of Entrance Island, are two nearly vertical standing logs that have fallen over the bank and onto a beach. A Mitchell Marker reflector is placed on one of these logs. It shows up well when illuminated at nighttime with a searchlight.

Note: Some vessels do not monitor their VHF radios for Securité calls. When approaching Entrance Island at night, it is sometimes a good idea to give a searchlight Securité. Cast the beam of a searchlight above the area of Whitestone Narrows to let vessels know you are near and about to transit Whitestone Narrows.

22. **Highwater Island Lighted Buoy 23 to Dirty Water Point:** With Highwater Island Lighted Buoy 23 well ahead of the vessel, change the course to port to head between Highwater Island and Highwater Island Lighted Buoy 23. This course change should be started when the vessel is abeam of the head of the unnamed indentation or cove in the Baranof shore immediately north of Highwater Island on the port side. Steady up on a course of 145 to 146 degrees true with Wyville Reef ahead. Look to the starboard for a reflector on a fallen tree on the Dirty Water Point shore.

    Note: Vessels skirt past the shoreline of Highwater Island on the port, but the Highwater Island shore drops off rapidly and the water is deep. The channel between Highwater Island and Highwater Island Lighted Buoy 23 is 125 yards wide.

    Note: Highwater Island once had a World War II check-in point and lookout post, but the structure is overgrown with young trees and is no longer visible.

23. **Dirty Water Point to Wyville Reef Lighted Buoy 22:** Change the course to starboard when the reflector on Dirty Water Point is well

Vessel congestion at Wyville Reef Lighted Buoy 22, Dirtywater Point, and Highwater Island in Neva Strait. PHOTO COURTESY OF CAPTAIN MATTHEW G. WILKENS.

forward of the starboard beam. Use a healthy amount of rudder to get the vessel turning to starboard. Once the vessel is swinging to starboard, ease off as needed and steady up on a course of 168 degrees true.

Prepare for the next course change at Wyville Reef Lighted Buoy 22 to the port. Some navigators use a course of 165 degrees true to favor the Wyville Reef Lighted Buoy 22 side of the channel. Be very cautious of bank suction and squat when transiting this shallow and narrow passage.

Note: This course change is critical and must be accomplished promptly to avoid advancing onto Wyville Reef.

Note: The Mitchell Marker on Dirty Water Point is on a fallen tree near the waterline.

Note: Dirty Water Point is named for the muddy waters that result from vessel wakes washing over the clay mud along the shoreline. This point is slowly eroding and is known for its toppled trees.

24. Wyville Reef Lighted Buoy 22 to Whitestone Narrows Buoy 17: Change the course to port when Wyville Reef Lighted Buoy 22 is forward of the port beam. Steady up on a course of 148 degrees true. This heading should be midchannel between Columbine Rock Buoy 20 and Columbine Rock Daybeacon 19. As before, use a healthy amount of rudder to get the vessel turning to port. Once past Columbine Rock, shape up the course to head on Whitestone Point ahead and to pass between red nun Buoy 18 and Whitestone Narrows Buoy 17. Set the radar VRM to 0.28 NM. When this ring touches Whitestone Point dead ahead, it is time to begin the next course change.

Whitestone Narrows

25. Whitestone Narrows Lighted Buoy 17 to Neva Point Light 12: When the 0.28 NM VRM ring touches Whitestone Point dead ahead, begin to change course to starboard with a moderate amount of rudder. Steady up on course 165 degrees true. This course will place a vessel on the Whitestone Narrows Range dead astern. This heading should be on the west tangent of Sound Island ahead or visually on the rock just north of Sound Island. Visually, this turn should begin just before Whitestone Narrows Buoys 17 and 13 on the starboard side line up with one another. It does not take a great amount of rudder, but do not delay the turn.

Pass through Whitestone Narrows, keeping the vessel as close to the range astern as possible. The range favors the starboard buoyed side of the channel. Continue on course 165 degrees true until past Whitestone Narrows Lighted Buoy 13. Once past, the water begins to deepen substantially and the vessel's speed may be increased if desired. At a small, unnamed point midway between Whitestone Point and Neva Point, some mariners like to change course to 153 degrees true to be heading on the east tangent of Sound Island. Be aware of the rock that bares 10 feet just north of Sound Island.

Note: There is a very shallow shoulder just at the turning point at Whitestone Narrows Lighted Buoy 17. This shoal is very near the middle of the channel with least depths of 22.5 feet. During periods of low water, a vessel may take a sheer to port when southbound. Be on guard for bottom suction, squat, and sheer. There is also a dangerous 11-foot shoal on the edge of the dredged channel immediately south of Whitestone Point Light 14 on the port side. This shoal shows kelp in the summer months.

Note: When looking aft to the Whitestone Narrows Range Lights astern, the front range light either right or left of the rear range light determines whether the vessel is to the right or to the left of the range line.

Note: It is approximately 40 minutes from Whitestone Narrows to the Alaska State Ferry Terminal.

26. **Neva Point Light 12 to Olga Point Light 11:** When Neva Point Light 12 is forward of the port beam broad on the bow, change the course to port with a moderate amount of rudder. Steady up on course 090 degrees true. This is a substantial course change, which should not be made lazily.

    Note: When emerging from Whitestone Narrows at Neva Point, on the starboard is a good view of Mt. Edgecumbe on Kruzof Island. To the port side is a spectacular view of Mt. Annahootz on Baranof Island.

Olga Strait

27. **Olga Point Light 11 to Creek Point:** Come nearly abeam of Olga Point Light 11 on the starboard side and change course to starboard with a moderate amount of rudder. Steady up on a course of 142 to 143 degrees true. This heading should be on the eastern

tangent of Krestof Island to pass midway between Creek Point on the port and the Krestof Island shore on the starboard.

28. **Creek Point to Olga Strait Light 9:** Change the course to port when Creek Point is forward of the port beam. Steady up on a course of 125 degrees true, heading on a small mountain saddle on the Halleck Island ridgeline ahead.

    Note: Begin to reduce speed again to pass Middle Shoal on the starboard side. A vessel can experience bottom suction, squat, and sheering to port when transiting at or near low water. Caution is advised.

    Note: A Mitchell Marker is placed on a tree on Creek Point. It is visible with a searchlight at night but hard to see during the day due to tree branch growth.

29. **Olga Strait Light 9 to unnamed rounded point on Halleck Island:** Begin changing course to the starboard when Olga Strait Light 9 is well forward of the starboard beam. Visually, start the turn when Olga Strait Light 9 and Olga Strait Light 7 line up, or set the VRM to 0.17 NM. When the VRM touches Olga Strait Light 9, begin the turn. Use a moderate amount of rudder. Come to course 144 degrees true, heading very near Olga Strait Light 5 in the distance ahead.

    Note: If it is near low water, reduce speed to half ahead or to a no-wake speed to avoid sheer and bottom suction, especially when passing Olga Strait Light 7. Speed can increase a short distance past Olga Strait Light 7 as the water begins to deepen.

    Note: Middle Shoal is 400 yards long along the axis of Olga Strait, with depths ranging from 18 to 22 feet and marked on each end with lighted aids to navigation on steel piling.

30. **Unnamed rounded point on Halleck Island to Olga Strait Light 5:** When abeam of the unnamed rounded point on Halleck Island, change the course slightly to port. Steady up on course 140

degrees true to pass midway between Olga Strait Light 5 and the Halleck Island shore.

31. **Olga Strait Light 5 to Eastern Point:** When past Olga Strait Light 5, change the course slightly to port to a course of 137 to 138 degrees true. This heading will be on the sharp point just south of Dog Point. The course passes along the Halleck Island shoreline, avoiding the offshore rock due east of Eastern Point covered by five feet of water. This unnamed rock shows kelp in the summer months.

32. **Eastern Point to Big Gavanski Island Light 3:** When Eastern Point opens up with the Siginaka Islands and you can see into Eastern Bay, begin to change course to 153 degrees true. Begin to reduce speed to a no-wake speed to pass safely by the float house community secured in the cove just south of Dog Point.

    Note: It is 20 minutes from Eastern Point to the Alaska State Ferry Terminal.

Starrigavan Bay

33. **Big Gavanski Island Light 3 to Alaska State Ferry Terminal:** If approaching the terminal dock for a starboard side landing, come nearly abeam of Big Gavanski Island Light 3 and steady up on a course of 143 degrees true on Harbor Point. Begin to slow down, making the approach on the dock when Old Sitka Rocks Light 2 is in the middle of the channel opening to the south. Set the VRM to 0.40 NM. When the variable range ring touches the beach ahead, change course to the port and make a safe approach to the dock.

    If approaching the terminal dock for a port side to landing, come to course 118 degrees true once past Lisianski Point Light 4 and head on the point where the Old Sitka State Historical Monument is located. Begin to slow down and make the approach, being sure to turn sharply to the dock once Old Sitka Rocks closes with the shoreline of Harbor Point.

Note: Be aware of the shallow water on the western end of the Alaska State Ferry Terminal dock. In times of westerly and northerly winds, set onto the dock can be very rapid.

Note: Anchorage can be found approximately 400 yards north of the Alaska State Ferry Terminal in 20 to 26 fathoms.

Peril Strait

Outbound from Sitka

Outbound from Sitka

Starrigavan Bay

1. **Alaska State Ferry Terminal to Big Gavanski Island:** After departing the ferry terminal port side to, come to a course of 315 degrees true, heading for a midchannel point northeast of Big Gavanski Island Light 3. After departing the ferry terminal starboard side to, come to a course of 305 degrees true, heading for a midchannel point northeast of Big Gavanski Island Light 3. Adjust the compass heading as necessary to be close to midchannel.

   Note: It is approximately 40 minutes to Whitestone Narrows from the Alaska State Ferry Terminal.

   Note: It is 154.0 NM to Petersburg, 152.0 NM to Buoy "WN" (the entrance to Wrangell Narrows), and 133.4 NM to the Alaska State Ferry Terminal at Auke Bay (Juneau).

Olga Strait

2. **Big Gavanski Island Light 3 to Eastern Point:** When Big Gavanski Island Light 3 is on the port bow, change course to the starboard and steady up on a course of 333 degrees true, passing Lisianksi Point Light 4 on the starboard side. This heading will line up in a prominent notch, notably visible on the radar, just to the west of Krugloi Point dead ahead.

   Note: When on this reach, it is not necessary to slow down for the float houses at the cove inside Dog Point on the starboard side. Land shelters these floating structures from wake damage by vessels outbound from Starrigavan Bay.

3. **Eastern Point to Olga Strait Light 5:** When the southernmost point of Eastern Point comes abeam, or just past abeam, begin to change course to the port and steady up on a course of 317 degrees true to pass between Olga Strait Light 5 and the southwest shore of Halleck Island. Pass approximately 0.20 NM off Eastern Point to avoid the rock covered with five feet of water just east of Eastern Point.

   Other methods for this course change:

   - Set the VRM to 0.70 NM or 0.60 NM when on a smaller vessel. When the VRM ring touches the prominent notch west of Krugloi Point, start the turn and come to 317 degrees true.
   - When the highest hill of Crosswise Island on the starboard hand is just forward of the starboard beam, begin the course change to 317 degrees true.
   - When Creek Point is seen between Middle Shoal Light 9 and Middle Shoal Light 7, start the turn to 317 degrees true.
   - At night, set the EBL to 317 degrees true. Change course to 317 degrees true when the EBL touches on the right side of Olga Strait Light 5.

   Note: Captain Tillman Dagle wrote, "From Eastern Point to Olga Strait Light 5, [the current] seems to set one way or the other; [the ship] gets [too] close on the starboard hand, southwest shore of Halleck Island."[81]

   Note: When making this turn, the unusually shaped Beehive Island is on the starboard side.

4. **Olga Strait Light 5 to the unnamed rounded point on Halleck Island:** When passing Olga Strait Light 5 on the port side, change the course slightly to the starboard to a course of 321 degrees true

81 Captain Tillman Dagle, Alaska Marine Highway System, personal unpublished piloting notes for Peril Strait, Neva and Olga Straits, c. 1970.

heading on Olga Strait Light 7. Olga Strait Light 7 and Olga Strait Light 9 should line up in range.

5. **Unnamed rounded point on Halleck Island to Olga Strait Light 9:** When abeam of the unnamed rounded point on Halleck Island, come slightly to the starboard to course 325 degrees true, passing one-third off the Middle Shoal side and two-thirds from the Halleck Island shoreline.

   Note: Prepare to reduce speed to a no-wake speed to avoid bottom suction and sheer, especially when passing Middle Shoal during times of low water. Warns Captain Dagle, "Between Olga Strait Lights 7 and 9 watch for set to starboard. Don't let this happen!"[82]

6. **Olga Strait Light 9 to Creek Point:** When abeam, or perhaps slightly before abeam, of Olga Strait Light 9, change the course to the port and steady up on a course of 305 degrees true passing midchannel between Creek Point and the northeast shore of Krestof Island. During an ebbing current, watch for set to the Krestof Island shore.

   Captain Dagle reminds us, "Stay midchannel!"[83]

   Note: If the current is flooding to the north, start the turn a little early to avoid being swept to the north toward the Halleck Island shoreline south of Creek Point. If the tide is ebbing to the south, use a generous amount of rudder to prevent the current from holding up the turn. Increase engine power as needed once past Olga Strait Light 9.

7. **Creek Point to Olga Point Light 11:** When abeam of Creek Point on the starboard side, or when the shoreline past Creek Point breaks into view, come to the starboard and steady up on a course of 325 degrees true.

82 Dagle, unpublished notes.

83 Dagle, unpublished notes.

Note: A Mitchell Marker on Creek Point is visible at night with a searchlight. It marks the point at which the course change to starboard should be made. During daytime it can be obscured by dense tree branch growth.

Note: When approaching Olga Point Light 11 at night, it is advisable to warn other vessels of your presence with a searchlight Securité by casting a searchlight beam above the area of Whitestone Narrows.

Note: It is approximately 10 minutes to Whitestone Narrows from Creek Point.

Note: If other traffic is transiting Whitestone Narrows southbound, the deep water at the entrance to Nakwasina Passage is a good location to wait as the other vessel or vessels complete their transit of Whitestone Narrows.

Captain Robert M. Johnson described his method for transiting Olga Strait:

> When on course 317 degrees true, run past Olga Strait Light 5 to the next point on Krestof Island, then change course to 325 degrees true to pass midway between Olga Strait Light 7 and the Halleck Island shore and tangent to the beach just right of Creek Point.
>
> At Olga Strait Light 7 change the course to the left to 320 degrees true, paralleling the line[up] of the Olga Strait Light 7 and Olga Strait Light 9, heading on the south-pointing tip of Creek Point. At Olga Strait Light 9, change course to the port smartly to 305 degrees true.
>
> When nearing abeam of Creek Point on the starboard side, change the course to the starboard and steady up on course 325 degrees true, heading on the left side of the hill north of Neva Point. This hill is obvious at night, as it projects above the radar shadow of the beach line.

> Creek Point is a great place to give a Securité call [and] slow down [to] await traffic that may be transiting through Whitestone Narrows.[84]

8. **Olga Point Light 11 to Neva Point Light 12:** Begin to make this turn to the port when Olga Point Light 11 is one point forward of the beam, or when the smaller island just north of Sound Island breaks free visually from Olga Point in the distance. Use a moderate amount of rudder and steady up on a course anywhere between 267 and 270 degrees true, heading for the base of the "Goose's Neck." This course will carry a vessel to a position 0.10 NM distance off Neva Point. On nights illuminated with bright moonlight, the ridge in the background on Partofshikof Island directly above Whitestone Narrows resembles a goose in flight with an outstretched neck. This profile is visible on all but the darkest nights.

   Note: Begin to reduce speed again to a no-wake speed to prepare for the transit of Whitestone Narrows.

Whitestone Narrows

9. **Neva Point Light 12 to Whitestone Narrows Buoy Lighted 17:** When 0.10 NM distance off and abeam of Neva Point Light 12 or slightly before abeam, come to the starboard with a moderate amount of rudder. This turn is made aggressively. During the turn, the Whitestone Narrows Range Lights become visible north of Whitestone Point. Swing until the ship is heading on Whitestone Narrows Buoy 13, regardless of the heading.

   On approach to Buoy 13, keep the Whitestone Narrows Range in view and gently come on range to 345 degrees true when the time is right. This method is easier and safer than doing a grand sweep around Neva Point to line up on the Whitestone Narrows

84 Captain Robert M. Johnson, Alaska Marine Highway System, personal unpublished piloting notes on Olga Strait, c. 1990.

Range. When doing a grand sweep, there is the danger of swinging too wide.

Captain Dagle advised to be careful not to overrun the range, and to change the course so as to be near on range, 342 degrees true.[85] The ship should be on range 345 degrees true by the time it passes Whitestone Narrows Lighted Buoy 13.

When visibility is reduced, steady up on course 333 degrees true, instead of 342 degrees true, setting the radar's VRM to 0.33 NM. When the 0.33 NM VRM ring is about to touch or touches Whitestone Narrows Buoy 13, it is time to change course to the starboard and get on the Whitestone Narrows Range 345 degrees true. This is handy should visibility be lost to fog or heavy snow.

Course 333 degrees true also keeps the vessel farther away from the shoreline between Neva Point and Whitestone Point. This method works only if the ship is turned aggressively at Neva Point. Once on the Whitestone Narrows Range, try to keep the range lights in sight and do what is necessary to stay on the range.

Note: A course of 333 and the VRM of 0.33 make a good memory aid.

Note: Captain Dagle advised, "Stay close to Whitestone Narrows Buoys 13, 15, and 17. Be on guard against any sudden sheer of the vessel, especially low water sheers to starboard."[86] The dangers of bank suction, squat, and sheer are not exaggerated, especially if a vessel is going too fast. Be on guard for bottom suction and sheer at all times, but especially during times of low water.

Note: There is a very shallow 22.5-foot shoulder just at the turning point at Whitestone Narrows Lighted Buoy 17 near midchannel. Be aware of a dangerous 11-foot shoal immediately to the south of Whitestone Narrows Light 14 on the very edge of the dredged channel on the starboard side. This shoal shows kelp during the summer months.

---

85 Dagle, unpublished notes.

86 Dagle, unpublished notes.

Neva Strait

10. Whitestone Narrows Lighted Buoy 17 to Wyville Reef Lighted Buoy 22: When transiting Whitestone Narrows on the range, adjust the radar VRM to 0.08 NM. When the VRM ring touches Whitestone Narrows Lighted Buoy 17, begin to turn to the port to course 328 degrees true with a moderate amount of rudder. This too is an aggressive turn.

"Keep a watch on red nun Buoy N 18," noted Captain Dagle.[87] Come to a course of 328 degrees true to pass midchannel between Columbine Rock Daybeacon 19 and Columbine Rock Buoy 20. An alternative is to let the ship swing past 328 degrees true and gently coax it back to 328 degrees true to be sure to clear the shoal marked by Buoy N 18. The 328 degrees heading is tangent to Dirty Water Point and favors the Baranof Island side of the channel.

Pass between Columbine Rock Daybeacon 19 and Columbine Rock Buoy 20. Once a vessel is past Columbine Rock Daybeacon 19, adjust the course to 327 or 326 degrees true, passing close to Wyville Reef Lighted Buoy 22 on the starboard side.

Note: Captain Dagle recommended, "Stay close on Wyville Reef Lighted Buoy 22 on the ebb tide [flowing to the north]. Use special care not to overrun Wyville Reef Lighted Buoy 22. On the flood tide [flowing to the south] use sufficient rudder to get your turn to starboard started."[88]

11. Wyville Reef Lighted Buoy 22 to Dirty Water Point: At Wyville Reef Lighted Buoy 22, change course to 345 degrees true. On the port hand at Dirty Water Point, look for the Mitchell Marker on a fallen tree along the Partofshikof Island shoreline, approximately 300 yards past Wyville Reef Lighted Buoy 22. This marks the point for the next course change.

This course should be initiated when Wyville Reef Lighted Buoy 22 is broad on the starboard bow. It is better to be a little early with this turn, slowing the swing down as the vessel swings

87 Dagle, unpublished notes.

88 Dagle, unpublished notes.

to the new heading of 345 degrees true. Most navigators favor the buoy side of the channel.

Note: The course changes at Wyville Reef Lighted Buoy 22 and Dirty Water Point are similar to skiing slalom with a large ship. No sooner does one steady up on course 345 degrees true when it is time to make the next course change to the port. These course changes are to be made not lazily but aggressively. In some cases, there is not time to steady up on course 345 degrees true; instead, swing past it and then swing immediately to the port to the next course of 325 degrees true.

12. **Dirty Water Point to Highwater Island Lighted Buoy 23:** When Dirty Water Point is forward of the beam, change the course to the port using a moderate amount of rudder. Steady up on a course of 324 to 326 degrees true, passing close by Highwater Island on the starboard hand. Highwater Island Lighted Buoy 23 will be close on the port side with the new heading slightly to the right of Highwater Island Lighted Buoy 23. Captain Dagle noted, "[at] the little mud slide on the port hand [Dirty Water Point], start your turn to port using sufficient rudder to get started. Change the course to 324 [degrees true]."[89] Be ready for a significant amount of bank suction, squat, and sheer when passing Dirty Water Point.

    Note: The water begins to deepen on the approach to Highwater Island.

13. **Highwater Island Lighted Buoy 23 to Entrance Island:** At Highwater Island Lighted Buoy 23, change course to the starboard and steady up on 335 degrees true. This is to avoid the rock outcropping approximately 800 yards north of Highwater Island along the Baranof Island shoreline. Once abeam of the rock outcropping 800 yards northwest of Highwater Island along the shoreline, adjust the course to the starboard, steadying up on course 338 degrees true. This is to avoid the rock covered by 14

89 Dagle, unpublished notes.

feet of water on the port side opposite Entrance Island. This rock is marked by kelp during the summer months. Captain Dagle commented, "Be aware of the rock outcropping 800 yards north of Highwater Island. Also be aware of the 2/2 fathom [2-fathom, 2-foot] area opposite . . . Entrance Island."[90]

14. **Entrance Island Light 24 to Scraggy Island:** The next course change is made 0.50 NM past Entrance Island. Watch for the west side of Scraggy Island to close in range with the west side of the Kane Islands. When these two shorelines are in range, it is time to change course. A Mitchell Marker indicates the course change position in a small bight southeast of Gilmer Cove. Two nearly vertical standing logs have fallen over the bank onto a beach. A reflector board on one of these logs shows up well when illuminated with a searchlight at night.

On the starboard side, a white outcropping of rock comes into view along the otherwise gray cliff shoreline of Baranof Island. When the white outcropping is broad on the starboard bow, it is time to change course. The most certain aid is to run past Entrance Island Light 24, set the VRM to 0.50 NM, and wait for it to touch Entrance Island as it passes astern. Whatever method is used, change course to port and steady up on a heading of 316 degrees true in order to pass approximately 0.10 to 0.12 NM east of Kane Island Light 25. When near Kane Island, keep in mind the rocks that lurk off the Baranof Island shoreline on the starboard side.

Note: The area between Kane Island and Scraggy Island is a good location to give a Securité call for Sergius Narrows.

Salisbury Sound

15. **Scraggy Island to Kakul Rock Lighted Buoy 2:** When abeam of the south end of Scraggy Island, change course to the starboard and steady up on a heading of 352 degrees true. This heading is on a

90 Dagle, unpublished notes.

prominent point dead ahead and just to the northeast of Round Island. Adjust the VRM to 0.60 NM. When the VRM ring touches the prominent point ahead, it is time to begin the next course change. Visually, look up Kakul Narrows to anticipate Channel Rocks Light 4 to open into view.

Note: A good swell from the Gulf of Alaska can roll well into Salisbury Sound, but the exposure to the swell is of short duration. However, if significant swell is rolling in, run out the course of 316 degrees true between Entrance Island and Scraggy Island in order to roll out on the next course of 037 degrees true to put the swell astern.

Note: It is approximately 15 minutes to Sergius Narrows from Scraggy Island.

Note: Fog can move into Peril Strait and Neva Strait from Salisbury Sound.

Kakul Narrows

16. Kakul Rock Lighted Buoy 2 to Channel Rocks Light 4: When the 0.60 NM VRM touches the prominent point northeast of Round Island, it is time to change course to the starboard and enter into Kakul Narrows. When the Channel Rocks Light 4 becomes visible, it is time to change course. When on a larger vessel after dark, wait to see one red flash of the Channel Rocks Light 4 before changing course.

Smaller vessels should wait for two red flashes of the Channel Rocks Light 4 before changing course. Use a moderate amount of rudder and steady up on a course of 037 degrees true. The heading should be on a small point of land projecting into Bradshaw Cove just to the north of Struya Point. This will carry a vessel midchannel through Kakul Narrows between Brad Rock and the Channel Rocks.

Note: Captain Dagle observed, "On the ebb tide when approaching the Channel Rocks Light, watch for set to the port toward Brad Rock."[91]

17. **Channel Rocks Light 4 to Struya Point:** Change course to the starboard when the Channel Rocks Light 4 is slightly forward of abeam, or as the light closes with the tangent of Range Point. Use a moderate amount of rudder and steady up on a heading of 076. This is called the Union 76 heading. The heading falls on the east tangent of Schulze Head dead ahead. Pass until abeam of Struya Hill on the port side or abeam of the small unnamed grass-covered rock just northwest of Range Point on the starboard side. This grass-covered rock makes a good radar image. The skyline of Struya Point is visible at night.

    Note: Whenever near Struya Point, Suloia Point, or Fish Bay, a navigator must be aware of the unmarked and dangerous Haley Rocks covered with four feet of water. They pose a substantial danger and remain unmarked by an aid to navigation.

    Note: When arriving early on the tide for Sergius Narrows, Fish Bay offers good anchorage to await the tide. The best anchorage is found at Haley Anchorage, 0.30 NM west of Haley Point. Depths range from 18 to 20 fathoms with a sandy bottom and good shelter from southerly winds. Great care must be taken to first avoid Haley Rocks when navigating in Fish Bay.

    Note: The shoulder extending to the south of Piper Island with a least depth of six fathoms (36 feet) was the anchorage used by Captain Harold Payne to await the Sergius Narrows tide if necessary. This location provides good holding ground.

18. **Struya Point to Suloia Point Light 5:** When abeam of Struya Hill or the bare grass-covered rock northwest of Range Point, change course to the port and steady up on 034 degrees true. This heading

91 Dagle, unpublished notes.

will be on Pinta Head. Another method is to wait for Suloia Point Light 5 to break open before making the turn. This method ensures that a vessel will be a little wider on Suloia Point and thus on the correct side of the channel since this is a blind corner.

Sergius Narrows

19. Suloia Point Light 5 to West Francis Rock Lighted Buoy 6: Come abeam of Suloia Point Light 5 and change course to the port using a moderate amount of rudder. Steady up on a heading of 350 to 355 degrees true to steer on the white spot midway between Point Sinbad and the unnamed point to the east. A heading of 350 degrees offers an easier approach with more room for turning. Set the VRM to 0.40 NM. Smaller vessels should adjust the VRM to 0.35 NM. When the VRM ring touches the shoreline ahead, east of Point Sinbad, begin to change the course to starboard for the transit of Sergius Narrows.

Note: Other visual aids to employ are Suloia Islet on the port hand and the bare rocks northwest of Pinta Head on the starboard hand. When abeam of these landmarks, it is time to change course to the starboard. Make this turn aggressively to avoid swinging wide when making the approach and lineup for transiting Sergius Narrows.

Note: When the 0.40 NM VRM touches Point Sinbad dead ahead, note that the VRM ring also simultaneously touches the small island just northwest of Pinta Head on the starboard side and Suloia Rock on the port side.

Note: Some change course to 069 to 072 degrees true when Liesnoi Shoal Buoy 10 opens into view from behind Rapids Island.

20. West Francis Rock Lighted Buoy 6 to Liesnoi Shoal Lighted Buoy 11: When the above VRM touches Point Sinbad, begin the starboard turn with a healthy amount of rudder and carefully gauge the rate of turn. Ease off on the rudder if necessary. There is a tendency to take the rudder off too soon due to the false impression

The M/V *Kennicott* outbound while passing between Sergius Narrows Buoy 8 and Sergius Point Light 9 at the beginning of a flood current. PHOTO COURTESY OF CAPTAIN MATTHEW G. WILKENS.

the vessel is coming around too fast, when in fact the ship is rapidly advancing toward the Chichagof Island shore. As Sergius Narrows Buoy 8 and Wayanda Ledge Buoy 10 come into range with one another, a swinging ship should be nearing the base course of 069 to 072 degrees true. This is a course change of 80 degrees or more.

Steady up on a heading of 069 to 072 degrees true. This heading should be very near on Liesnoi Shoal Lighted Buoy 11 ahead in the distance. Travel through Sergius Narrows, passing between Sergius Point Light 9 and Sergius Narrows Buoy 8. Most mariners tend to favor the buoyed side of the channel. Once past Wayanda Ledge Buoy 10, change course slightly to the starboard, steadying up on a heading of 074 degrees true. This will allow a vessel to pass Liesnoi Shoal Lighted Buoy 11 ahead on the port side. Be aware of the submerged rock off Shoal Point.

Note: Captain Dagle cautioned, "Give West Francis Rock Buoy 6 a fairly wide berth and due regard for the newly reported hazards in the West Francis Rock area. Bottom is foul ground. Stay mid-channel between Sergius Point Light 9 and [Sergius Narrows] Buoy 8. At [Wayanda Ledge Buoy 10], change to the starboard to 074 [degrees true]."[92]

Note: Slow down a little to transit Sergius Narrows. The old-timers always recommended keeping some reserve power in your back pocket in case of need.

Note: If any ebb current is present, it generally flows with the axis of the channel. Upwelling and swirls occur north of West Francis Rock Lighted Buoy 6 to Point Sinbad on ebb currents.

If any flood current is present, expect turbulent water and a set to the left. Upwelling and swirls occur between Wayanda Reef Buoy 10 and Liesnoi Shoal Lighted Buoy 11 on flood currents.

21. **Liesnoi Shoal Lighted Buoy 11 to Point Siroi Light 12:** When Liesnoi Shoal Lighted Buoy 11 is broad on the port bow, change course to the port and steady up on a heading of 043 degrees true. Try to maintain a distance of 0.10 NM off Mountain Head and Liesnoi Shoal Lighted Buoy 11. This heading should be inside Middle Point ahead, with Point Siroi coming up on the starboard side. Be cautious of meeting opposing traffic between Mountain Head and Liesnoi Shoal Lighted Buoy 11. The distance off Point Siroi should be at least 0.12 NM.

22. **Point Siroi Light 12 to the little islet off Big Island:** When Point Siroi Light 12 is forward of the starboard beam, or abeam, change the course to the port and steady up on 034 degrees true. The heading should be slightly inside Middle Point ahead.

23. **The little islet off Big Island to Middle Point Light 14:** When abeam of Bear Bay Island on the starboard or Grasstop Rock in

92 Dagle, unpublished notes.

the entrance of Deep Bay on the port, prepare for the next course change to the port. Do not start the course change before abeam of the Deep Bay Entrance Daybeacon 1 perched on top of Grass Top Rock. Begin changing course to 000 degrees true when Grasstop Rock comes in line with Grasstop Island. Some like to come nearly abeam of the little islet off Big Island before changing course to port and steadying up on a due north heading of 000 degrees true. This heading should be on the east tangent of Arthur Island dead ahead. When making this course change, be aware of the 19-foot depth just east of the little islet off Big Island.

Note: Captain Dagle used a slightly different method for this course change, writing, "Bear Bay Island or Grasstop Rock in mid channel Deep Bay, start change to port and steer just to the right of Arthur Island 002 [degrees true]. Keep in mind the shoal and foul ground just off [the] S.E. end of [the] little island off Big Island."[93]

24. **Middle Point Light 14 to Yellow Point Light 16:** When Middle Point Light 14 is broad on the starboard bow, change course to the starboard and steady up on a heading of 034 degrees true. This heading will be well inside Rapids Point ahead. Regard the covered 12-foot shoal just south-southeast of Arthur Island one-third the distance across the channel.

Adams Channel

25. **Yellow Point Light 16 to Big Rose Island Light 21:** Visually, when Yellow Point Rock Daybeacon 18 closes with the beach on the starboard hand, begin to change course to the starboard, using a moderate amount of rudder. An alternative is to change course when Yellow Point Light 16 is broad on the starboard bow or when it is in range with Yellow Point Rock Daybeacon 18. Steady up on a heading of 080 degrees true.

93 Dagle, unpublished notes.

At night and with the radar, when the point of land just west of Yellow Point Rock Daybeacon 18 begins to show on the radar behind Yellow Point, it is time to change course to the starboard and steady up on 080 degrees true. This heading is to the left of an unnamed creek dead ahead pouring into the Adams Channel, marked with a white fisheries marker. Keep to the midchannel and regard the shallow mudflats at the mouth of Range Creek on the starboard side.

26. **Big Rose Island to Nixon Shoal:** This is a large and sweeping course change to come around Big Rose Island in Adams Channel. Begin this turn when abeam of the southwest point of Big Rose Island on the port hand. Use moderate amounts of rudder while gauging the turn to stay in midchannel.

It is preferable to be more left-handed than right-handed when making this turn. Observe Light 19 closely in order to keep a safe distance. As a general rule, be 0.08 NM off Rose Island Rock Light 19 and finish the turn 0.08 NM off Big Rose Island.

Nearing Big Rose Island Light 21, steady up on a course of 345 degrees true. This heading should line up on the unnamed easternmost point on the Chichagof Island shoreline dead ahead to remain midchannel and well clear of Nixon Shoal on the port hand.

Note: The channel east of Big Rose Island is the Adams Channel. The channel to the west is the Rose Channel. Smaller vessels hoping to avoid traffic in the Adams Channel can use the Rose Channel.

Note: Avoid meeting other vessels before committing to the turn at Big Rose Island.

27. **Nixon Shoal to Flat Point Light 22:** Nixon Shoal is a low, grass-covered gravel bar on the starboard side along the Baranof Island shoreline, and it can be difficult to see either visually or by radar at night, especially during times of high water. Come to the starboard when Nixon Shoal is slightly forward of the starboard

beam and steady up on course 354 degrees true. This heading should be just inside Pogibshi Point ahead with Flat Point Light 22 fine on the starboard side.

28. **Flat Point Light 22 to Povorotni Island Light:** When Flat Point Light 22 is well forward of the starboard beam, change course to the port and steady up on course 338 degrees true to pass mid-channel between Povorotni Island and the Chichagof Island shoreline. This heading is tangent to the point on the north side of Poison Cove. Vessels should pass more to the Baranof Island side to avoid the large and growing stream delta on the Chichagof Island side.

Deadman Reach

29. **Povorotni Island Light to Hoggatt Reef Light 25:** When abeam of the Povorotni Island Light or when the light is just forward of the beam, change course to the starboard, keeping the Povorotni Island Light abeam during the course change. Begin with a moderate amount of rudder. Maintain a distance of approximately 0.25 NM off the north side of Povorotni Island. Steady up on a heading of 054 degrees true. This heading should be on Otstoia Island Light dead ahead in the distance. When transiting through Deadman Reach, set the VRM to 1.90 NM to prepare for the next course change at Hoggatt Reef Light 25.

30. **Hoggatt Reef Light 25 to Elovoi Island Light 26:** When the 1.90 NM VRM ring touches the southwestern end of Otstoia Island dead ahead, change the course to the port. Visually, change course when the vessel is abeam of the east end of Hoggatt Island on the port hand. Another visual method is to wait until Hoggatt Reef Light 25 is abaft the port beam. This course change is gradual. Steady on a course of 012 degrees true and maintain a distance of 0.55 NM off Hoggatt Island. On the starboard side, maintain a distance of 0.45 NM off the southwest end of Krugloi Island.

Note: Hoggatt Island is a very low and flat island that makes a poor radar target. Hoggatt Reef Light 25 does make a radar target but is not a good turning point for this course change unless it is past abeam on the port quarter. It is best to use the 1.90 NM VRM method mentioned above.

31. **Elovoi Island Light 26 to Broad Island Light:** Come abeam 0.55 NM off the north end of Elovoi Island. Change the course to the starboard, keeping the Elovoi Island Light 26 abeam 0.55 NM. Steady on a course of 085 degrees true. Ushk Point should be astern and the vessel should pass Broad Island 0.35 NM off on the port side.

32. **Broad Island Light to False Lindenberg Head:** When passing Broad Island Light 0.35 NM off on the port side on course 085 degrees true, continue until abeam of the eastern end of Broad Island. Change course to the starboard and steady on a heading of 130 degrees true, keeping the Broad Island Light nearly astern, or the middle of Broad Island astern. Maintain a distance of 0.80 NM off the Point Benham Light. This is the longest reach in Peril Strait at 12.2 NM long. Maintain a distance of 0.70 NM off False Lindenberg Head. This heading is on the left tangent of the island to the northeast of Dead Tree Island.

    Note: At Broad Island, it is 116.0 NM to Petersburg, 114.0 NM to Buoy “WN” (the entrance to Wrangell Narrows), and 95.5 NM to the Alaska State Ferry Terminal in Auke Bay.

33. **False Lindenberg Head to McClellan Rock Light:** Come abeam of False Lindenberg Head 0.70 NM off. Change course to the port and steady up on a heading of 108 degrees true to be 0.50 NM off the McClellan Rock Light. This heading is on the right tangent of Eva Island. A visual method is to watch for Fairway Island Light 32 to line up with McClellan Rock Light when off False Lindenberg Head, and then to change course to 108 degrees true.

34. McClellan Rock Light to Morris Reef Lighted Buoy 35: Come abeam of the McClellan Rock Light with a 0.50 NM distance off. Change course to the port and steady up on 085 degrees true, passing 0.50 NM off Fairway Island Light 32 on the starboard side. Pass 0.70 NM off the Point Craven Light and 0.50 NM off the Morris Reef Lighted Buoy 35 on the port side.

Note: Do not get closer than 0.80 NM from the south Baranof Island shore here without plotting the ship's position. There is much foul ground between Fairway Island and Svensen Rock.

If southbound in Chatham Strait when exiting Peril Strait, set up the radar cursor or index line to a heading of 145 degrees true. When this line touches the unnamed peninsular point separating Florence Bay from Sitkoh Bay on the port hand, change course to the starboard and steady on a heading of 145 degrees true. This course change point is nearly midway between Fairway Island Light 32 and the Morris Reef Lighted Buoy 35 and will allow a vessel to clear Midway Reef 0.80 NM on the starboard side. The unnamed peninsular point separating Florence Bay from Sitkoh Bay should fall directly astern when on the new heading. Pass Point Thatcher at 1.25 NM distance off. From Point Thatcher, adjust the course for southerly headings in Chatham Strait.

If northbound in Chatham Strait when exiting Peril Strait, continue on course 085 degrees true until abeam of the Morris Reef Lighted Buoy 35. Maintain a 0.50 NM distance off the buoy. Round the buoy slowly to the port, maintaining a distance of 0.50 NM off the buoy. Steady up on a course of 007 degrees true to pass Peninsular Point 1.40 NM distance off. When abeam of Peninsular Point, adjust the course for northerly headings in Chatham Strait.

When approaching Chatham Strait, take care to avoid the extensive Morris Reef complex of ledges and submerged rocks southeast of Point Hayes if exiting the entrance to the north and the smaller Midway Reef if exiting to the south.

A line from Morris Reef Lighted Buoy 35 to the tangent of Peninsular Point passes along the eastern edge of Morris Reef. This makes a good danger bearing. It is advisable to stay well away from this line of danger. Most of the foul ground lies to the west of the line, but some is also just to the east of it.

Bear in mind that it is risky business to use a floating aid to navigation because the buoy may shift position. A radar cursor or index line should be set for the new heading of 007 degrees true to pass Peninsular Point 1.4 distance off as a safety measure.

Peril Strait

Sitka Sound Routes

Sitka Sound Routes

Big Gavanski Island Light to Sitka Harbor or to the Eastern Anchorage near Jamestown Bay via the Western Channel

1. **Big Gavanski Island Light 3 to Old Sitka Rocks Light 2:** If inbound for Sitka Harbor or the Eastern Anchorage near Jamestown Bay, come abeam of Big Gavanski Island Light 3 and change course to the starboard. Steady up on a course of 190 degrees true to pass Old Sitka Rocks Light 2 on the port side.

   Note: Between Harbor Point and Old Sitka Rocks Light 2, you can see the Old Sitka Dock cruise ship dock. Large cruise ships arrive and depart from this location in the summer months.

2. **Old Sitka Rocks Light 2 to Halibut Point:** Come abeam 0.20 NM off Old Sitka Rocks Light 2 and change course to 163 degrees true for the south end of Halibut Point. Maintain a distance off Halibut Point of at least 0.20 NM.

3. **Halibut Point to the unnamed rounded point northwest of Watson Point and the islet south of Apple Island:** When abeam of the south end of Halibut Point, change course to the port and steady up on a heading of 147 degrees true. Be aware of the foul ground that shoals to five feet and eight feet, respectively, marked by Kasiana Island Shoal Buoy 1, north of the east side of Kasiana Island. On the port side, come abeam of an unnamed rounded point northwest of Watson Point along the Baranof Island shore. Maintain a distance of 0.20 NM off this point. Note also that on the starboard side, the small islet south of Apple Island, just south of Kasiana Island, is abeam at 1.00 NM distance off.

Note: Smaller vessels can set an inbound course for Sitka Harbor from here, but regardless of size, if traveling to the Eastern Anchorage, continue on to Makhnati Rock Buoy 2 by way of the Western Channel.

4. **Unnamed point northwest of Watson Point to Makhnati Rock Buoy 2 via the Western Channel:** When abeam of the unnamed point northwest of Watson Point, change course to the port and steady up on a course of 202 degrees true. When on course 202 degrees true, this unnamed point should fall in directly astern of the vessel. Pass Battery Island marked by the Battery Island Light 6 at 0.20 NM off on the port side and the Usher Rock Shoal Lighted Buoy 5 close on the starboard side. Be aware of the covered three-foot rocks just north of Signal Island on the east side of the channel, nearly opposite the Usher Rock Shoal Lighted Buoy 5. Beyond Usher Rock Lighted Buoy 5, pass Signal Island Light 4 with a distance of 0.20 NM off, or slightly less on the port side.

   Note: Use NOAA nautical chart 17327 for more detail.

5. **Makhnati Rock Buoy 2 to Eckholms Island Light:** Come abeam of the Makhnati Rock Buoy 2 and maintain a distance of at least 0.30 NM off. Come around the buoy easy while making the course change. Steady up on a course of 125 degrees true. This puts the Eckholms Island Light on the starboard side. Set the VRM to 0.40 NM. When the ring touches the Eckholms Island Light, it is time to change course for Tsaritsa Rock Lighted Buoy 7. On the port side, a vessel should be abeam of the southeasternmost islets of the Kayak Islands at the beginning of this course change.

6. **Eckholms Island Light to Tsaritsa Rock Lighted Buoy 7:** As the 0.40 NM VRM ring touches the Eckholms Light, and when abeam of the southeasternmost islet of the Kayak Islands on the port side, change course to the port and steady up on a heading of 084 degrees true. This heading will pass 0.20 NM off the Tsaritsa Rock Lighted Buoy 7. A vessel should be 0.25 to 0.30 NM off the

Eckholms Light when on the new heading of 084 degrees true. Pass Simpson Rock Lighted Bell Buoy 5 on the port side, approximately 0.20 NM distance off. Begin to reduce speed. A vessel should be at half speed by the time it reaches Tsaritsa Rock Lighted Buoy 7.

7. **Tsaritsa Rock Lighted Buoy 7 to Twins Light 9:** Round Tsaritsa Rock Lighted Buoy 7, maintaining a 0.20 NM distance. This may take a large amount of rudder for a larger vessel. Reduce speed to slow ahead by the time the vessel passes Rocky Patch Lighted Buoy RP on the starboard side. Steady up on a course of 024 degrees true. This heading should be on the eastern or right tangent of Cannon Island at the entrance to Jamestown Bay. Maintain a distance off the Twins Light 9 of approximately 0.15 NM.

   Note: Stay wide on the Twins Light 9 during an ebb tide. The set on the ebb is toward the west and the Twins.

8. **Twins Light 9 to the seven-fathom anchorage in the Eastern Anchorage:** When nearly abeam of the Twins Light 9, change course to the port, steadying up on a heading near 353 degrees true to be heading on the mouth of the Indian River ahead. Slow down to dead slow ahead and prepare for anchorage. Set the VRM to 0.30 NM. When this VRM ring touches Cannon Island, the vessel is then over the seven-fathom bank. Let go four shots of anchor chain on deck.

   Note: A shiphandler can also proceed straight ahead, steering on the eastern or right tangent of Cannon Island at the entrance of Jamestown Bay. Anchorage is found in 21 fathoms 0.33 NM from Cannon Island ahead and 0.33 NM off Ring Island. Let go six shots of anchor chain.

   Note: When at anchor, the large tank on the south end of Japonski Island and the Mt. Edgecumbe Hospital on Japonski Island should be viewed between the towers of the Sitka-Mt. Edgecumbe Bridge.

The Eastern Anchorage near Jamestown Bay to Big Gavanski Island Light via the Western Channel

9. **Seven-fathom bank in the Eastern Anchorage to Twins Light 9:** When departing the Eastern Anchorage, maintain a distance off the Twins Light 9 of approximately 0.15 NM. Watch for set to the west if departing on an ebb tide.

10. **Twins Light 9 to Tsaritsa Rock Lighted Buoy 7:** When approaching the Twins Light 9, begin turning to starboard before abeam of the light. Use a large amount of rudder and steady up on a course of 205 degrees true. This heading will lead to a position of approximately 0.20 NM distance off the Tsaritsa Rock Lighted Buoy 7. The vessel will pass the Rocky Patch Lighted Buoy RP on the port side. Begin to build up the vessel's speed.

11. **Tsaritsa Rock Lighted Buoy 7 to Eckholms Light:** When changing course, round the Tsaritsa Rock Lighted Buoy 7 from a distance of 0.20 NM. It may take a large amount of rudder for a larger vessel. Maintain a distance off the buoy of 0.20 NM when coming around. Steady up on a course of 264 degrees true, passing the Simpson Rock Lighted Bell Buoy 5 on the starboard side at approximately 0.20 NM distance off. This heading will lead to a distance off the Eckholms Light of 0.30 NM.

12. **Eckholms Light to Makhnati Rock Lighted Buoy 2:** When the Eckholms Light is still forward of the port beam, begin the turn to the starboard. Steady up on a course of 305 degrees true in order to pass with a 0.30 NM distance off the Makhnati Rock Lighted Buoy 2.

13. **Makhnati Rock Lighted Buoy 2 to unnamed point northwest of Watson Point and Kasiana Island:** Round the Makhnati Rock Lighted Buoy 2 easy and maintain a distance of 0.30 NM when coming to port. Enter into the Western Channel rounding Makhnati Rock Buoy 2, heading between Signal Island Light 4 and Sentinel Rock to pass the Usher Rock Shoal Buoy 5 on the port side. Steady up on a course of 022 degrees true.

Pass the Signal Island Light 4 at 0.20 NM, or slightly less, on the starboard side. Be aware of the three-foot-deep covered rocks just north of Signal Island on the east side of the Western Channel, nearly opposite the Usher Rock Shoal Lighted Buoy 5.

Pass the Usher Rock Shoal Lighted Buoy 5 close on the port side. Pass Battery Island marked by the Battery Island Light 6 at a distance of 0.20 NM off on the starboard side. The unnamed point northwest of Watson Point will be dead ahead when on this heading.

14. **Kasiana Island and unnamed point northwest of Watson Point to Halibut Point:** Adjust the VRM to 0.40 NM. When the VRM ring touches the unnamed point northwest of Watson Point ahead, it is time to begin changing course to the port. Visually, Old Sitka Rocks will close with Halibut Point. On the port side, a vessel will pass abeam of the south end of Kasiana Island. Come around with a moderate amount of rudder and steady up on a heading of 327 degrees true to pass Halibut Point at a distance of 0.20 NM on the starboard side. Be aware of the foul ground north of the east side of Kasiana Island that shallows to five feet and eight feet, marked by Kasiana Island Shoal Buoy 1.

15. **Halibut Point to Old Sitka Rocks Light 2:** Come abeam of the south side of Halibut Point and change course to the starboard. Steady up on a heading of 343 degrees true to pass 0.20 NM off Old Sitka Rocks.

16. **Old Sitka Rocks Light to Big Gavanski Island Light 3:** When abeam of Old Sitka Rocks Light 2, change course to 010 degrees true to pass Big Gavanski Island Light 3 at a distance of 0.20 NM off on the port side. The Lisianski Point Light 4 should be showing dead ahead or slightly on the port side. From Old Sitka Rocks Light 2, a vessel can also maneuver into Starrigavan Bay and the Alaska State Ferry Terminal.

Note: Between Harbor Point and Old Sitka Rocks Light 2, you can see the Old Sitka Dock cruise ship dock. Large cruise ships arrive and depart from this location in the summer months.

Cape Edgecumbe to the Eckholms Light

17. Cape Edgecumbe Light to Vitskari Island Light: When entering Sitka Sound from the Gulf of Alaska, maintain a distance off Cape Edgecumbe of at least 3.20 NM. As the ship comes around with Cape Edgecumbe 3.20 NM to the north, steady up on a heading of 076 degrees true with the Kulichkof Rock Lighted Bell Buoy 2 dead ahead. Pass St. Lazaria Island on the port side with a distance of at least 1.30 NM off. This heading will lead to a distance of 1.00 NM off the Vitskari Island Light.

Vitskari Island Light is unusual in having the only RACON (radar beacon) in Southeastern Alaska, showing RACON: Morse code O (— — —). These three bright dashes on the radar help the navigator determine Vitskari Island Light's range and bearing.

Note: In the summer months, this area can be heavily congested with numerous salmon trollers and charter sportfishing vessels. Vessels may have to pass wider than 1.3 miles off St. Lazaria Island to avoid the trollers and sport fishers. Adjust the course as necessary to arrive at Vitskari Island Light with a distance off the light of 1.00 NM.

18. Vitskari Island Light to Kulichkof Rock Lighted Bell Buoy 2: Come abeam of the Vitskari Island Light 1.00 NM distance off. Change course to the port and steady up on a heading of 062 degrees true to pass 0.50 NM to the north of the Kulichkof Rock Lighted Bell Buoy 2.

Note: In the summer, numerous trolling vessels may be found in this area, making it difficult to see the Kulichkof Rock Lighted Bell Buoy 2 visually. The same is true on the radar due to the many trolling vessels speckling the screen. Set the radar cursor or index line to a heading of 082 degrees true, which is the next course at

Kulichkof Rock Lighted Bell Buoy 2. As the cursor or index line touches Vitskari Island Light when passing it on the port side, change the course to 082 degrees true.

19. **Kulichkof Rock Lighted Bell Buoy 2 to Eckholms Light:** As the cursor or index line touches with Vitskari Island Light as mentioned above, change course to the starboard and steady up on a heading of 082 degrees to pass 0.30 NM off the Eckholms Light. Maintain a distance of 0.50 NM off Kulichkof Rock Lighted Bell Buoy 2.

Eckholms Light to Cape Edgecumbe Light

20. **Eckholms Light to Kulichkof Rock Lighted Bell Buoy 2:** When making the entrance into Sitka Sound from the Eastern Anchorage, come abeam of the Eckholms Light 0.30 NM distance off. Change course to 262 degrees true. This heading will be on the Vitskari Island Light dead ahead to pass 0.50 NM north of the Kulichkof Rock Lighted Buoy 2.

21. **Kulichkof Rock Lighted Bell Buoy 2 to Vitskari Island Light:** When the Kulichkof Rock Lighted Bell Buoy 2 is abeam on the port side, 0.50 NM distance off, or Vitskari Island Light is 3.00 NM ahead, change course to the port and steady up on course 242 degrees true to pass 1.00 NM off Vitskari Island Light.

22. **Vitskari Island Light to Cape Edgecumbe Light:** When 1.00 NM off Vitskari Island Light, change course to the starboard and steady up on a course of 256 degrees true. This heading will pass St. Lazaria Island at a distance of 1.30 NM off on the port side 3.20 NM off the Cape Edgecumbe Light as the ship enters the Gulf of Alaska.

    Note: In the summer months, the course may need to be wider on St. Lazaria Island and Cape Edgecumbe due to the numerous commercial salmon trollers and charter fishing vessels that may be encountered.

Vitskari Island Light to Big Gavanski Island Light and Starrigavan Bay

Note: The track up the coast on the outside of Baranof Island from Cape Ommaney to Biorka Island is 324 degrees true to pass 5.00 NM off Cape Ommaney and 4.50 NM off Biorka Island.

Note: When abeam of Biorka Island 4.50 NM off its western shore, change the heading to 354 degrees true, steering on St. Lazaria Island ahead. When St. Lazaria Island is 6.30 NM ahead, change course to starboard and steady up on a heading of 040 degrees true to pass Vitskari Island Light 1.00 NM on the port hand. This is done to avoid Biorka Reef, off the northwestern shore of Biorka Island.

23. **Vitskari Island Light to Bieli Rocks:** Change course to port by rounding Vitskari Island 1.00 NM off on the port side. Maintain the distance of 1.00 NM as the ship comes around. Steady up on a heading of 355 degrees true to pass Bieli Rocks 1.00 NM off on the starboard side.

24. **Bieli Rocks to northwestern point of Middle Island:** When abeam of Bieli Rocks, change course to the starboard and steady up on a heading of 029 degrees true to pass 0.80 NM off the northern end of Crow Island on the starboard side. When abeam on the starboard side of the northwestern point of the larger Middle Island, change the course again to the starboard, steadying up on a heading of 064 degrees true.

25. **Northwestern point of Middle Island to Big Gavanski Island Light 3:** When changing the course to starboard, steady up on a heading of 064 degrees true to pass approximately midway between the Siginaka Islands and Big Gavanski Island. The Lisianski Point Light 4 should be dead ahead. Pass approximately 0.30 NM off the western shore of Big Gavanski Island.

    Note: When approaching Big Gavanski for the next course change, either to the port into Olga Strait or to the starboard and into Starrigavan Bay, be aware that Lisianski Peninsula is closing rapidly dead ahead. Make the course change promptly, using a moderate amount of rudder. Watch for cross traffic in Olga Strait. Reduce speed to make this course change to prevent advancing rapidly toward the Lisianski Peninsula shore.

26. Big Gavanski Island Light 3 to Alaska State Ferry Terminal: Round Big Gavanski Island at least 0.25 NM off. If approaching the terminal dock for a starboard side landing, come nearly abeam of Big Gavanski Island Light 3 and steady up on a course of 140 degrees true. Begin to reduce speed, making the approach on the dock when Old Sitka Rocks Light 2 is in the middle of the channel opening to the south. Another aid is to set the VRM to 0.40 NM. As the VRM ring touches the beach ahead, change course to the port and make a safe approach on the dock.

If approaching the terminal dock for a port side to landing, come to course 118 degrees true once past Lisianski Point Light 4. Head on the point where the Old Sitka State Historical Monument is located. Begin to slow down to make the approach, being sure to turn sharply to the dock once Old Sitka Rocks closes with the shoreline of Harbor Point.

Note: Be aware of the shallow water on the western end of the Alaska State Ferry Terminal dock. In times of westerly and northerly winds, set onto the dock can be very rapid.

Note: Anchorage can be found approximately 400 yards north of the Alaska State Ferry Terminal in 20 to 26 fathoms.

Starrigavan Bay to Big Gavanski Island and Vitskari Island Light

27. Alaska State Ferry Terminal to Big Gavanski Island: After departing the ferry terminal port side to, come to a course of 315 degrees true, heading for a midchannel point northeast of Big Gavanski Island Light 3. After departing the ferry terminal starboard side to, come to a course of 305 degrees true, heading for a midchannel point northeast of Big Gavanski Island Light 3. Adjust the heading as necessary to be close to midchannel. Come to Big Gavanski Island Light 3 on the port side approximately 0.25 NM off.

28. Big Gavanski Island Light 3 to the northern end of Crow Island: Round Big Gavanski Island and steady up on a heading of 244 degrees true in the middle of the channel between Big Gavanski Island and the Siginaka Islands. This heading places the Lisianski Point Light 4 dead astern. On this heading, a vessel should pass Big Gavanski Island on the port side, approximately 0.30 NM off. Come abeam of the northern end of Crow Island just past the northwestern point of Middle Island.

29. Northern end of Crow Island to Bieli Rocks: When abeam of the northern end of Crow Island, change the course to the port and steady up on a heading of 209 degrees true. A vessel should be approximately 0.80 NM off Crow Island. This heading takes the ship to Bieli Rocks. Run past abeam of Bieli Rocks approximately one point abaft the port beam to make the next course change to Vitskari Island.

30. Bieli Rocks to Vitskari Island Light: When Bieli Rocks are one point abaft the port beam, change course to the port and steady up on a heading of 175 degrees true to pass Vitskari Island 1.00 NM off on the starboard side. Maintain a distance of 1.00 NM off when rounding the island. Change the heading for both St. Lazaria Island and Cape Edgecumbe, or alternatively for Biorka Island and Cape Ommaney.

Vitskari Island to Makhnati Rock Buoy 2 and the Western Channel

31. Vitskari Island to Makhnati Rock Buoy 2 (if using the Western Channel): When inbound from the Gulf of Alaska and abeam of Vitskari Island, come to a heading of 051 degrees true. This will take a vessel to a point 0.30 NM off the Makhnati Rock Buoy 2 with Signal Island Light 4 nearly dead ahead. While entering into the Western Channel, set the VRM at 0.30 NM to preserve a distance of 0.30 NM off Makhnati Rock Buoy 2. As the 0.3 VRM ring touches Signal Island ahead, change the course to the port and steady up on a heading of 022 degrees true. This heading will pass

Signal Island Light 4 0.20 NM on the starboard side and Usher Rock Shoal Buoy 5 on the port side.

32. **Makhnati Rock Buoy 2 to Vitskari Island, when exiting the Western Channel:** Run past Signal Island Light 4 on the port side. Change course to the starboard, maintaining a distance of 0.30 NM off the Makhnati Rock Buoy 2, and steady up on a heading of 231 degrees true. This heading will pass Vitskari Island 1.00 NM off on the starboard side.

Wrangell Narrows

Introduction to Wrangell Narrows

Wrangell Narrows is found in the heart of Southeastern Alaska. Southeast's Inside Passage is configured much like an hourglass. Both its northern and southern reaches have wide and deep straits, with the Wrangell Narrows constriction point in the middle. For regular users of Southeast Alaska's waterways, the narrows cannot be ignored.

The narrows have been nicknamed Pinball Alley, Christmas Tree Lane, the Twisting Nightmare, and the Ditch. Irrespective of nicknames, viewing Wrangell Narrows from the bridge of a ship for the first time is an intimidating sight. The scene is filled with numerous blinking and fixed lights, day beacons, ranges, unlighted buoys, mudflats, boulder fields, rocks, strong currents, and islets close by the narrow channel.

Wrangell Narrows has been said to be the most buoyed channel in the world. As a measure of assurance, the 1917 *United States Coast Pilot* noted that the extensive system of lights, beacons, and buoys, "with the aid of a chart, render the navigation of the narrows fairly easy for small craft, even without local knowledge." This holds true in the present day. However, vessels with more than ten feet of draft are strongly advised to hire a local pilot.

This navigable waterway demands immense respect from marine navigators of the Inside Passage. "I've lost a lot of hair over the years," quipped Captain Thomas Aspinwall. "Wrangell Narrows has scalped a lot of us. The rocks are just outside the wheelhouse windows."[94] Guiding a ship or pulling a barge through the narrows is precision work, especially during periods of reduced visibility. There are times when you can see absolutely nothing in the narrows due to dense fog or heavy snow presenting the additional danger of spatial disorientation. If you have any misgiving about reduced visibility in Wrangell Narrows, call the 24-hour desk with the National Weather Service in Juneau at (907) 790-6800. A meteorologist on duty can predict to almost within an hour when reduced visibility will dissipate.

The greatest navigational risks to ships result from confined geography, heavy traffic, and reduced visibility. All three can occur simultaneously in Wrangell Narrows. A private report conducted by Arthur D. Little, Incorporated, in July 1991 stated, "Wrangell Narrows is the single area in all of Alaska that has the most incidents and stands out as a high risk area."[95]

This section is an attempt to describe navigating Wrangell Narrows. It is hoped that this information is helpful and practical for navigators who travel through the narrows. It is further hoped that this will be used as an aid to learning more about this intricate waterway.

The information contained herein represents years of accumulated knowledge by masters and pilots of the Alaska Marine Highway System. It is written for general interest only and is not intended to be the complete, definitive, and specific rule or method for the navigation of Wrangell Narrows. It does not supersede or contradict information found within the *Coast Pilot*, applicable charts, or any official government publications and documents that pertain to navigation of this area.

It is the responsibility of each individual vessel master to exercise proper judgment with regard to due diligence and to the practice of good seamanship. These duties appropriately rest upon each vessel master.

94 Captain Thomas Aspinwall, personal communication, Ketchikan, Alaska, c. 2010.
95 Alaska Regional Response Team: www.akrrt.org/SEAKplan/SEAKbackgrnd.shtml, accessed September 2001.

Navigating Wrangell Narrows

To the navigator, there are several Wrangell Narrows to know intimately. The northbound passage is different from the southbound passage. Wrangell Narrows must be known both by the navigator's eye and by the radar image view. It is critical to correctly interpret what is seen on the radar screen when visibility is lost due to heavy snow, darkness, or fog. A master of Wrangell Narrows, Captain Harold Payne, once said, "Anyone can run a ship through the narrows on a good day and a good tide. But try it in the snow."[96]

> The *United States Coast Pilot 8, Pacific Coast Alaska: Dixon Entrance to Cape Spencer* states: "specific courses for Wrangell Narrows would be of little help and could be confusing." Much of the knowledge of navigating Wrangell Narrows has been passed down orally from the time of the Alaska Steamship Company and earlier. With each passing generation, some of this knowledge is lost.
>
> Steve Pierce, a resident of Island Point along Wrangell Narrows writes:
>
> > Before living on the Narrows, I had no idea how complex the area really is. Every little bight was at one time an Indian fish trap site, and the remains of those are easily found. There were at one time over 100 fish processing facilities (mostly

96 Joel W. Rodgers, "Alaska By Ferry," *Alaska Airlines Magazine*, February 1981.

> salteries) on the Narrows.... Island Point was named in 1884 by a U.S. Navy Survey crew led by Comdr. J.B. Coghlan, who noted "there is an island off the point." Well, that island is where our cabin is located, and about 250 feet up the beach, at what we call our "Little Cabin." There is low ground that used to cover at some high waters, thus making an island of the tip of the point. Apparently, isostatic rebound from the last Ice Age has allowed the land to rise to the point that this phenomenon [of Island Point becoming an island at high tide] no longer happens, even on storm tides.[97]

During the Ice Age, immense weight from ice depressed the earth's crust. Long after the ice retreated, the crust is slowly rebounding upward. Due to this geologic process, Wrangell Narrows is becoming shallower as time goes on.

To obtain a feel for Wrangell Narrows and to gain some historical perspective, it is beneficial to see what has been written about this area in the past. We are fortunate to be able to do this with past editions of the government-published *United States Coast Pilot.* The United States government has published the *Coast Pilot* for Southeast Alaska since 1869, shortly after the US purchase of Alaska from Russia in 1867.

In the 1869 *Coast Pilot of Alaska, First Part, from Southern Boundary to Cook's Inlet,* by George Davidson, assistant coast survey, we can read a short description of "Wrangell Strait," as it was then called. Much of Davidson's data for this edition came from Russian sources. Quoting this classic volume:

> It would serve no practical purpose to endeavor to describe the intricacy of islands and sounds south of Frederick Sound and east of Chatham Strait. The maps that are already published are good guides for all general purposes. There is

97 Steve Pierce, email correspondence, March 24, 2007.

> only one available channel between Clarence and Frederick Sounds east of Coronation Island, and that is Wrangell Strait, opening from the northwestern part of Stikine Sound, in latitude 56 degrees 35 minutes and longitude 132 degrees 48 minutes. It bears north-northeast, distant four miles from the east end of the large island lying in the middle of the west entrance of Stikine Sound. It is tortuous, very narrow, has low wooded shores, broad beaches, and a mid-channel depth of not less than four or five fathoms. A sketch of this, on a large scale, is given on sheet No. 106 of the Russian charts of the Pacific Ocean series. This sketch is not very accurate, but it can be used, especially at low water, when a few rocks not laid down upon it show themselves. The United States steamer Saginaw and other government steamers have used it.

Notice that before there were aids to navigation, it was recommended to transit Wrangell Narrows on a low tide to be able to observe hazards not visible at high tide.

The 1883 *Pacific Coast Pilot—Alaska, Part 1* contains a more extensive description of Wrangell Strait that runs six pages. However, there is a degree of uncertainty contained in the description:

> The next navigable passage northward from Sumner Strait is Wrangell Strait, named and first surveyed by the Russians. It was entered by one of Vancouver's boat parties, but reported by them to be impassable on account of shoal water and in fact to terminate in a cul-de-sac.
>
> The several charts are very discrepant in this vicinity. Three plans of the strait have been published, one by the Russian Hydrographic Office, No. 1441, in 1850, from surveys by Lindenberg

in about 1838, and one by the U.S. Hydrographic Office, sub-sketch on No. 225, in 1869, from a reconnaissance made by Messrs. Bridge, Pillsbury and Schroeder, of the U.S.S. Saginaw, R.W. Meade, Jr., commanding, on March 20 and 21, 1869. A third, No. 713, above mentioned, has recently been issued by the U.S. Coast Survey from a reconnaissance made by the naval officers on the U.S. Coast Survey steamer Hassler in 1881. This contains numerous important additions and corrections, and together with notes submitted by Lieut-Commander H.E. Nichols, U.S.N., commanding, has formed the basis of the following

The M/V *Kennicott* passing Burnt Island northbound. This section of the waterway is where the original name of Wrangell Narrows was first applied. COURTESY OF CAPTAIN WILLIAM M. HOPKINS.

> description. It must be borne in mind, however, that a thorough and final survey has yet to be made.
>
> The channel usually followed lies between Burnt Islet and the shore to the eastward; it is very narrow between Burnt Islet reefs and the foul ground making off fifty yards from the Mitkoff Shore. The clear channel appears to be less than two cables in width. This locality is that commonly known to local navigators as Wrangell Narrows.

Regarding Danger Point, we read:

> At this point the channel is a short cable wide and requires circumspection in its use.
>
> In Wrangell Strait most of the dangers are uncovered at low water, and at high water are marked by kelp, which, however, probably disappears during the winter season.
>
> Wrangell Strait is not considered a dangerous passage by Meade or Nichols; there are no short turns nor very bad tides, but a stranger should not attempt the passage except at low water, when nearly all the dangers are visible. The best stage of the tide to make the passage from either entrance is at a quarter flood.

By 1891, the beginning of an aid-to-navigation system is found. The 1891 *Pacific Coast Pilot—Alaska, Part 1, Dixon Entrance to Yakutat Bay With Inland Passage From Strait of Fuca to Dixon Entrance* has four pages of description, including sailing directions with aids to navigation. At this time, the waterway was still called Wrangell Strait.

> This is a narrow, somewhat tortuous, navigable channel connecting Sumner Strait with Frederick Sound. Its southern entrance is about 19 miles west from Wrangell, and it is the passage now

> generally used by vessels plying between the south and Sitka.
>
> In June, 1890, the Pacific coast steamship *Queen,* having a length of 341 feet and drawing 20 feet when loaded, under command of Captain James Carroll, passed through Wrangell Strait without difficulty.
>
> Its general direction is true N. and S., and it lies between Mitkof Island on the E. and Woewodski Island and Lindenberg Peninsula (of Kupreanof Island) on the W. It is 20 miles in length, while the width from shore to shore varies from ¼ to ¾ of a mile. The channel is, however, contracted at various points, which render its navigation difficult, and even impossible, at low water, for vessels drawing more than 10 feet. It is, however, well buoyed, and marked by beacons, and is visited each season by the Inspector of the 13th Light House District, to examine and renew the aids to navigation.
>
> Navigators are particularly cautioned not to place too much dependence on the positions of the various buoys, as the strong currents, ice, and driftwood are liable to move them out of position or carry them away. The beacons are also liable to be carried away by ice and strong currents. The inspector of the Thirteenth Light House District usually makes an inspection here in July or August of every year.

In the 1917 *United States Coast Pilot—Alaska, Part 1, Dixon Entrance to Yakutat Bay,* the name Wrangell Narrows replaces Wrangell Strait for the entire length of the passageway. A table of courses and distances is also included in this edition.

> The channel is narrow and intricate in places, between dangerous ledges and flats, and the tidal

> currents are strong. It is marked by an extensive system of lights, beacons, and buoys, which, with the aid of the chart, render the navigation of the narrows fairly easy for small craft, even without local knowledge. Vessels of more than 10 feet draft, however, are advised not to attempt to go through without a pilot.
>
> The least depth in the channel is about 11 feet, on the middle ground northeast of Bayou Point.

The narrows were yet to be dredged at this time.

> The aids to navigation are placed for vessels going north; they are generally well preserved, but occasionally some of them are displaced or carried away by rafts, or drift in the strong currents, and this should be kept in mind, especially in the narrower parts of the channel. They are inspected about every five days or oftener, and if found out of position are replaced as soon as practicable.
>
> Vessels too large to make the passage through Wrangell Narrows safely continue westward through Sumner Strait, round Cape Decision, and go northward through Chatham Strait, or westward to sea by way of Cape Ommaney. Smaller vessels regularly using Wrangell Narrows sometimes use the longer passage to their advantage when not favored by suitable conditions of tide or daylight in the Narrows.

Petersburg is mentioned as a small fishing village with a cannery and post office. The town had radio communication to Wrangell.

The 1932 *United States Coast Pilot—Alaska* reads similarly to the 1917 edition; however, there are changes, including a more extensive description of Petersburg, tow channel regulations, and how parts of the channel have been dredged.

> The courses and distances through Wrangell Narrows are given in tabulated form on page 12. The short courses will only apply to small vessels since large vessels will cover a good part of the distance in making the turns. In some cases with twin screw vessels the engines are reversed in order to help make the sharp turns. Inquiry of local pilots showed that they did not use courses in the narrows because of strong currents and sharp turns. In foggy weather vessels come to anchor at either end of the narrows and wait until the fog clears away. Strangers may find that the large number of aids in the narrows is confusing and such persons will find the tabulated courses useful in keeping in the proper channel. Vessels of over 10 feet draft are advised to take a pilot.
>
> Wrangell Narrows has been improved to secure a channel 200 feet wide and 21 feet (6.1 m) deep at mean lower low water with increased depth in rock. This was obtained, but some of the cuts have shown a tendency to fill and considerable dredging has been required to maintain the 21-foot (6.1 m) project.
>
> Wrangell Narrows is well lighted throughout its length. The dredged channel is marked by lighted beacons, those on the western side of the channel having green lights with black day marks, and those on the eastern side of the channel having red lights with red day marks.

The 1990 *United States Coast Pilot 8, Pacific Coast Alaska: Dixon Entrance to Cape Spencer* is surprisingly similar in some respects to the 1932 edition. However, within it is a more detailed description of Petersburg, weather, regulations, and services.

The most important improvement concerns the dredged channels. "The Federal Project for Wrangell Narrows provides for several dredged sections 24 feet deep through the narrows, except for a dredged section W of Turn Point that has a project depth of 27 feet." (See the "General" section for depths in Wrangell Narrows.) The width of the channel through the various dredged sections is seen to have increased from the 200 feet of 1932 to 300 feet. *Local Notices to Mariners* should be consulted regularly for the latest information on the controlling depths.

The British Hydrographic Office's *Southeast Alaska Pilot, From Dixon Entrance to Cook Inlet* (1993) states:

> The navigator would pay close attention to the chart as the narrows are well marked with aids to navigation that should be closely followed. The channel throughout Wrangell Narrows is marked by an extensive system of lights, beacons and buoys (shown, as with most of the dangers, only on the national large scale chart). These aids are numbered: from 1 to 61 on the W side and exhibit port hand daymarks; and, from 2 to 62 on the E side and exhibit starboard hand daymarks.

The northern entrance is marked with a Safe Water buoy called the North Entrance Lighted Bell Buoy "WN." This was formerly Buoy 63. It is red-and-white striped with a red spherical topmark and a Morse (A) white flashing light. "WN" is the only buoy of its type in Southeast Alaska.

Wrangell Narrows is defined in the *Dictionary of Alaska Place Names* as follows:

> Wrangell Narrows: *water passage,* extends south 24 miles from Frederick Sound to Sumner Strait, separates Mitkof Island from Kupreanof and Woewodski Island, Alexander Archipelago; 56 degrees 31 minutes North, 132 degrees 55 minutes West; *BGN 1917*; (map 6). *Variants:* Proliv Vrangelya, Wrangell Strait.

> This feature was named "Proliv Vrangelya," or "Wrangell Strait," in 1838 by Lindenberg for Adm. Baron Ferdinand Petrovich von Wrangell; name published in 1850 on Russian Hydrographic Department Chart 1441. The name "Wrangell Narrows" was originally applied to the central part of Wrangell Strait where it is most constricted.

Many have wondered why this waterway is called Wrangell Narrows when the town of Petersburg is located on the north end of the narrows. Consulting the *Dictionary of Alaska Place Names* reveals the reason. The naming of Wrangell Strait in 1838 by Ivan Vasilevich Lindenberg, a Finnish seafarer and Russian American Company surveyor, predates the founding of Petersburg by 59 years. The town of Wrangell on Wrangell Island was originally founded as a fort in 1834 by then Russian Governor Wrangell to prevent the encroachment of Hudson Bay Company traders via the Stikine River onto Russian territory.

Sometime between 1897 and 1899, the town of Petersburg was founded by and named for Peter Buschmann. Petersburg was located at the northern entrance to Wrangell Narrows because of its close proximity to Le Conte Bay and a ready supply of icebergs that were used by the canneries before refrigeration.

You might ask why ships traverse Wrangell Narrows when there are other alternatives. Dry Strait, which borders the east side of Mitkof Island across the delta of the Stikine River from the mainland, has adequate depth for only small draft vessels at high tides. To the west of Wrangell Narrows is Keku Strait. However, this passage is too narrow and rocky to be of any use for vessels of larger draft and length. (Locally, Keku Strait is called Rocky Pass.)

The remaining alternative is to navigate Sumner Strait to Cape Decision, enter Chatham Strait to Kingsmill Point, and then turn east into Frederick Sound. This is the route of the large cruise ships or tugs towing tandem tows. It is 40.3 nautical miles from Wrangell and Petersburg via Wrangell Narrows and nearly 200 nautical miles from Wrangell to Petersburg via Sumner Strait,

Cape Decision, Kingsmill Point, and Frederick Sound. Over the course of a year, traveling via Wrangell Narrows saves much fuel consumption and running time. It is worth the time spent waiting for favorable tides and weather.

Another frequent question concerns the size of vessel that can safely transit Wrangell Narrows. This is difficult to answer with certainty, but analyzing regular users reveals an answer. Vessels are measured with various particulars. The overall length and tonnage are the main indicators of a vessel's size. The table below shows some of the largest vessels to use Wrangell Narrows in recent years.

From these examples, we can see that the Alaska Marine Highway System's M/V *Columbia* is the largest vessel in tonnage to use Wrangell Narrows on a regular basis, followed by the M/V *Kennicott.* However, the French cruise ship *L'Austral* is the longest vessel to use Wrangell Narrows.

The M/V *Frank H. Brown* and the M/V *Klondike*, of the White Pass and Yukon Railroad Corporation's former Ocean Division, were certainly large for Wrangell Narrows. With superstructures aft, these ships carried large gantry cranes forward of the wheelhouse for loading and unloading cargo containers. Having the capacity to hold 200 25-foot-long cargo containers, the *Brown* and *Klondike* carried a layer of cargo containers on top of the hold hatch covers. Up to 930,000 gallons of refined petroleum products were transported in the forward tanks and the wing tanks. At 20' 01"[98] these ships had the deepest mean draft of vessels known to use the narrows.

The cruise ship M/V *Song of Flower* claimed to be the largest vessel to transit Wrangell Narrows, but the following table shows this was not the case. However, it is true that the ship was difficult to handle, with twin propellers and a single rudder configuration.

The height of the tide, and therefore the depth of the water, must be taken into consideration to enter Wrangell Narrows with

98 Ship model of the M/V *Frank H. Brown* with vessel particulars and details at the Skagway, Alaska, office and museum of the White Pass and Yukon Railroad.

Vessel	International Tons	LOA*	Breadth	Draft	Propeller	Rudder
L'Austral	10,700	**466′**	59′	15′ 00″	2 CP*	Twin Becker*
Seaborn Pride	9,975	439′	63′	18′ 00″	2 CP	Twin
Columbia	**13,009**	418′	**85′**	17′ 07″	2 CP	Twin
Matanuska	9,214	408′	74′	17′ 00″	2 CP	Twin
Malaspina	9,121	408′	74′	16′ 11″	2 CP	Twin
Song of Flower	8,283	407′	53′	16′ 05″	2 CP	Single
Hanseatic	9,325	403′	59′	15′ 08″	2 CP	Twin
Frank H. Brown	6,900	394′	70′	**20′ 01″**	Twin	Twin
Kennicott	12,635	382′	85′	17′ 06″	2 CP	Twin Becker
Taku	7,302	352′	74′	16′ 11″	2 CP	Twin

* CP = controllable pitch propeller.
* Becker is a rudder with an additional, movable flap on the trailing edge, much like a trim tab on an airplane for greater maneuvering capability.
* LOA = length overall.
Numbers in bold indicate largest.

a deeper draft vessel. This is why depth limits are set for a ship. The amount of water depth above the charted datum or depths published on the nautical chart is called the tidal holdover.

Masters may employ holdovers of between two and five feet, individualized by vessel. A navigator must obey this limit religiously. When a ship passes through a shallow and narrow channel, it will sometimes begin to "smell the bottom," or squat. This is because in shallow water the stern will squat as it settles into the trough behind the bow wave, thus increasing the draft. A stern can be much closer to the bottom than is realized. A holdover is determined to avoid squatting in a shallow waterway.

Squat is a function of the depth and width of the channel, the beam of the vessel, block coefficient, and speed. The greater the speed in shallow water, the deeper the stern will sink. When a ship exceeds the critical speed, the bow will rise upward on a bow wave. The stern, in contrast, will sink quickly into a trough, thus reducing the clearance under the keel.

Squatting is greatly increased in shallow water due to the flow of water under the ship and the short distance to the bottom. This phenomenon is dangerous to the control of the ship and can produce sluggishness in answering the helm, resulting in yawing. This increases the potential for a vessel to sheer sideways in the channel. When this happens, the ship is reacting to very shallow water and excessive speed.[99] Squatting also increases wake size, resulting in damage to property along the shoreline.

To avoid this problem, masters should transit the narrows according to the limits imposed by a holdover and, above all, slow down. The holdover is the minimum depth at which the narrows should be transited at a safe speed. The tide should be at the proper holdover height or greater before transiting the narrows. Conversely, enough time should be allowed for a ship to complete the transit before this minimum water depth is reached with a

99 A thorough discussion of squatting is found in Russell Sydnor Crenshaw, *Naval Shiphandling* (Annapolis, MD: Naval Institute Press, 1974), 182–186.

falling tide. The greater the holdover depth used makes a shorter window of time for transiting the narrows.

On April 17, 2005, a boulder 19 feet below the charted depth was discovered by the US Army Corps of Engineers between Light 10 and Daybeacon 10A. The boulder was blasted in 2007, and the danger was removed. The finding of this boulder reinforces the wisdom of employing a holdover, not only to avoid squat but also to avoid any undiscovered and unpleasant surprises remaining on the bottom of Wrangell Narrows.

Captain Maynard Reeser once served as a pilot for an arrogant cruise ship captain. When the captain asked why Captain Reeser was afraid to enter into the narrows below a certain depth, Reeser replied, "It is not that I am afraid, but rather it is because I have more sense than to try it."[100]

Steep banks line the narrows in many places. A ship will indicate when it is getting too close to an embankment. A wedge of water between the bow and a steep bank will tend to push the bow off and draw the stern in.

In the rare manuscript *Ship Handling—Destroyers*, Admiral John W. Schmidt, US Navy, writes, "What flying speed is to an airplane, steerage way is to a ship. When she is moving through the water, you have control of her."[101] However, there are limits to speed in a narrow channel for the sake of avoiding squatting and controlling the ship and wake damage to property along the shoreline.

Shiphandlers must not risk losing control of the ship by going faster than they can think. This is what is meant by staying below a vessel's critical speed. Schmidt cautions, "The speed to choose in negotiating the channel depends on existing conditions, your common sense and harbor regulations."[102]

Since the 1990s, there has been much new home construction along the length of Wrangell Narrows. The factors of wake swell damage and speed for safe steering must be considered. Schmidt

---

100 Author's personal recollection.

101 John W. Schmidt, *Ship Handling—Destroyers* (US Navy, c. 1950), VII-1.

102 Schmidt, *Ship Handling*, VII-1.

points out, "It is your speed through the water, rather than engine speed, which creates the damaging swell."[103] In Wrangell Narrows, unless regulations otherwise prohibit it, a safe steering speed is all-important. Knowledge of an individual ship's behavior must be understood. Schmidt reminds us, "It should never be forgotten that the slower the speed, the more allowance you must make for the set of a constant current."[104]

Skill in conning the vessel cannot be overemphasized. When giving commands, the voice must be clear, calm, and authoritative. As a rule, a helmsman should be given a compass course rather than a mark on which to steer. The points given below support this policy:

- "It is easier for a helmsman to keep his mind on the compass card than on a landmark. He has no excuse to let his eyes wander, to 'rubber-neck' when he should be thinking of steering the ship."[105]
- "If the current is setting athwart the channel, you are not likely to notice it as quickly when steering for a mark, as if a compass course were being steered. That is, the helmsman heading toward a mark will steer a kind of spiral. If you give him a compass course, and then see that you are being set athwart the channel, all you have to do is give the helmsman a new course, adding a degree or two to the old one, or subtracting a degree or two, to bring you back [to the middle of the channel]."[106]
- "There can be poor visibility ahead, so that the helmsman cannot keep a mark continuously in view. People and things tend to get in his line of sight."[107]

---

103 Schmidt, *Ship Handling*, VII-2.
104 Schmidt, *Ship Handling*, VII-5.
105 Schmidt, *Ship Handling*, VII-5.
106 Schmidt, *Ship Handling*, VII-5.
107 Schmidt, *Ship Handling*, VII-5.

- When conning a ship, it is critical to stand on or near the centerline in order to observe the set of the vessel by the current. A navigator's position should be near the helmsman for ease of communicating the conning orders and with hands close by the engine controls.

In Wrangell Narrows visibility is often hampered by dense fog. There are times when you can see absolutely nothing in the narrows due to dense fog and/or heavy snow, presenting the additional danger for spatial disorientation. Until you have a thorough understanding of Wrangell Narrows by experience, avoid Wrangell Narrows during dense fog.

In fog, our perceptions and sensations may give us false information. Trust the radar. Using the radar is recommended even on the good days. Know and understand the radar image thoroughly. Do not use electronic charting for navigation, but do use it for confirmation of a vessel's position in the narrow channel.

The reasons for fog in Wrangell Narrows are important to understand. Meteorologist Robert Kanan, a 40-year veteran with the Juneau Office of the National Weather Service, explains:

> Petersburg and Wrangell Narrows is a real fog hole, often fogging earlier, lasting longer, and having lower visibility than areas nearby. During the rainy season of August through October, there is lots of low-level moisture available. All it takes is a very light wind to set off a fog event. Partial clearing will allow radiation cooling to quickly reach the dew point temperature and start the fog. But, even with cloudy skies the cooling from cold air drainage, primarily from the glaciers on the east side of Frederick Sound, takes place with the typical light northeast drainage winds during night time hours. That is why Petersburg, and the northern part of the Narrows, usually fogs in first. If there is a strong high-pressure area aloft, there also will be downward motion (subsidence) that

> helps hold the low-level moisture (marine stratus and fog) near the surface. This downward, or capping, motion is the main ingredient needed for a widespread and long duration fog event. Solar radiation from the sun is largely reflected off the top of a thick fog layer. To dissipate fog, heating near the surface must take place. This is why the fog burns off first over the land areas. Fog also dissipates from mixing warmer air into the layer, usually from an increase in the low-level winds.[108]

From *Ship Handling—Destroyers,* we read further:

> When you arrive at the entrance [to Wrangell Narrows] and it is shut in by fog, you are faced with a decision that all shipmasters must face many times in their careers. The decision to make is whether to go in or whether to anchor or jog outside and wait for the fog to lift. You are in the horns of a dilemma. If you decide to stay out at anchor or jog, you seem to be timid. If you go in and arrive safely, that is what is expected; and if you go in and have an accident in the fog, people will say you are a fool. In making your decision, you must take into account the urgency of your business, the ease with which the channel can be negotiated, the degree with which you are familiar with the channel, the probable amount of traffic to be expected...[109]

You must also consider how well your ship handles, and so on. Schmidt cautions, "Probably the most weighty factor in making your decision is your confidence in your own ability to make your way in a fog and in the ability of your crew to back you up."[110]

---

108 Robert Kanan, email correspondence, January 10, 2000.

109 Schmidt, *Ship Handling,* XV-1, 2.

110 Schmidt, *Ship Handling,* XV-2.

Currently, post-*Exxon Valdez,* a navigator will never be faulted for being cautious. Much depends on a captain's mood, temperament, and level of confidence.

One of the most revered masters to sail with the Alaska Marine Highway System, retired Captain Harold Payne, wrote: "Regarding fog in Wrangell Narrows and Sergius Narrows, my biggest worry is other vessels. You know what you are going to do, but you never know about [the intentions of] other vessels unless good radio contact has been made. Using a fine-tuned radar that picks out all the aids [to navigation] is absolutely necessary to keep going."[111] With his fingers crossed to signify good luck, Captain Payne said, "Some days are like this."

Wrangell Narrows is no place for second-guessing. When asked how he navigated the M/V *Taku* through Wrangell Narrows in dense fog, Captain Herb Houtary said, "I go by the numbers."[112] After several hundred round-trips, you get to a point where you expend little mental energy thinking about the numbers; they are ingrained in procedural memory, taking you to a higher level and experience.

There is an old saying in Southeast Alaska: "Anytime it is blowing southeasterly 25 knots and raining, a vessel can travel anywhere." That is largely true. Southeasterly winds from weather fronts moving onshore keep the fog away.

The Alaska Marine Highway System has been in full operation since 1963, when the first mainliner ferries were delivered to the State of Alaska. The system has maintained a commendable safety record. There have, however, been some incidents in Wrangell Narrows and other areas. These act as a reminder that no mariner is immune from mishap. Nevertheless, if certain rules are strictly followed, and vigilance is maintained, the probability of an accident is reduced.

- "When approaching the Petersburg terminal on April 26, 1963 during a minus tide of –3.4 feet, the M/V *Taku* had an

111 Captain Harold Payne, personal communication, January 6, 1990.

112 Captain Herb Houtary, personal communication, c. 1978.

8' x 70' section of her bottom pushed up. The charts showed a depth of 24 feet and the vessel drew 15 feet [at the time]."[113]

- "A report was issued on May 8 that stated a rock was found by the U.S. Coast Guard five feet above the channel controlled depth of 24 feet in Petersburg harbor. As the large rock was not shown on the charts, it was thought it may have been deposited from an iceberg stuck in the vicinity earlier in the year."[114] At the early stages of AMHS operation, there were no holdovers established. This incident revealed the need to have tidal holdovers in order to transit Wrangell Narrows. It also pointed out the danger of glacial icebergs. The rock, dubbed locally Taku Rock, was moved. At low tide, divers attached cables from a barge to the rock. As the tide rose, the rock was lifted simultaneously with the barge and was then deposited outside the channel limits.[115]

- On August 17, 1963, while the *Taku* was moored to the dock in Petersburg, two boys from San Diego pushed down on live throttles on the starboard bridge wing, causing the ship to lurch forward suddenly and powerfully. Damage to the dock was extensive, pulling down the two transfer bridge towers with the transfer bridge falling into the water. Repairs were not completed until two months later.[116]

- "On September 26, 1964 the M/V *Matanuska* struck a submerged object in Wrangell Narrows. Three of the four propeller blades and the shaft of the starboard propeller were bent."[117]

- In the 1960s, the M/V *Malaspina* lost all power between Light 18 and Light 16 while southbound against a flood current.

113 Betz, "Ferries in the North," 55.

114 Betz, "Ferries in the North," 55, 56.

115 Shelly Pope, "AMHS Celebrates 50 Years in Southeast," *Petersburg Pilot* XXXIX, no. 18 (May 13, 2013): 4.

116 Pope, "AMHS Celebrates 50 years in Southeast," 4.

117 Betz, "Ferries in the North," 59.

Malaspina had to drop both anchors until the problem was repaired. Fortunately, this was accomplished before the current changed direction.[118]

- On February 22, 1976,[119] "the M/V *Columbia* brushed the bottom in Wrangell Narrows because of an electrical failure in the wheelhouse to the steering gear. The vessel veered hard to port,"[120] struck the beach, and damaged one ballast tank.[121] This incident occurred at Battery Islands while the ship was northbound. Suffering a mechanical difficulty is one of the greater risks when navigating Wrangell Narrows.
- On March 29, 1978,[122] the M/V *Malaspina* struck Light 31 southbound in Wrangell Narrows while avoiding a northbound fishing vessel in dense fog. As mentioned above, it is vital to establish clear communication between vessels. "The Captain was blamed by the USCG . . . [for excessive speed] . . . in heavy fog, with limited visibility."[123]
- On June 15, 1978,[124] the southbound M/V *Aurora* met the northbound M/V *Taku* at Light 25 in Wrangell Narrows. The *Aurora* pulled over to the far starboard side of the channel to get out of the *Taku*'s path, scraping Light 25. This left a 60' gash in the hull where a large number of transverse frames were creased on the starboard side of the *Aurora*'s car deck. This incident was a result of poor communications and timing between the two vessels. Ample room for safe passage was available south of Light 25. This was the "second ferry to hit a channel marker in three months."[125]

---

118 Captain Harold Payne, personal communication, 1986.
119 Alaskan Shipwreck Database: www.mms.gov/alaska/ref/ships, accessed in 1999.
120 Betz, "Ferries in the North," 66.
121 Alaskan Shipwreck Database.
122 Alaskan Shipwreck Database.
123 Alaskan Shipwreck Database.
124 Alaskan Shipwreck Database.
125 Alaskan Shipwreck Database.

- On January 15, 1982, the tanker/freighter M/V *Frank H. Brown* ran aground in Wrangell Narrows, spilling 32,631 gallons of gasoline.[126] The ship's deep draft made it difficult to navigate through the narrows. It should have gone around Cape Decision, avoiding Wrangell Narrows altogether because of its draft and dangerous cargo.
- In April 1987, the tug *Roughneck,* towing the barge *Annahootz* northbound, fetched up on the sandspit on Mitkof Island behind Light 32A. The *Roughneck,* underpowered and with a single screw, could not control the barge. The *Annahootz,* which was carrying both freight and fuel, was an unwieldy barge and did not pull straight, yawing back and forth. At Buoy 29, the *Annahootz* veered with a mind of its own out of the channel toward Mitkof Island. The *Annahootz* dragged the *Roughneck* along as it departed the channel and grounded on the sandspit. There was no spillage of fuel.
- On January 20, 1990, the tanker/freighter M/V *Frank H. Brown* grounded at Green Rocks while northbound in Wrangell Narrows, spilling 1,286 gallons of gasoline.[127] This came 10 months after the *Exxon Valdez* oil spill, and it marked the end of the *Frank H. Brown*'s career. Thereafter it was converted into an uncrewed barge, sailing the route under tow from Vancouver to Skagway for a short time, and then disappeared into history.
- In 1990, the Coast Guard Cutter *Sweetbrier* departed Scow Bay with a lazy turn to the north, then struck the mud and boulder flats south of Light 52. As a result, Daybeacon 51A was constructed.[128]

---

126 Alaska Regional Response Team: www.akrrt.org/SEAKplan/SEAKbackgrnd.shtml, accessed in 1999.

127 Alaska Regional Response Team: www.akrrt.org/SEAKplan/SEAKbackgrnd.shtml, accessed in 1999.

128 Captain Alan Doty, personal communication, 1999.

- In the early 1990s, the Coast Guard Buoy Tender *Planetree* turned too soon southbound at Light 4A, striking its port side on the rock ledge immediately to the south of Light 4A off Battery Islet. The No. 1 hold was torn open and flooded, but the watertight bulkheads and watertight doors held.[129]
- In May 1991, the M/V *Columbia* was southbound between the Flats. A northbound light aluminum skiff hit the *Columbia*'s wake at high speed, capsizing and spilling the skiff's two occupants into the water. The *Columbia* turned around near Papke's Landing and recovered the two people. There was one fatality.
- On May 28, 2003, the M/V *Columbia* suffered a generator fire at Light 52 southbound in Wrangell Narrows. It was a fortuitous location as *Columbia* was able to anchor in nearby Scow Bay.
- On June 3, 2003, while northbound in dense fog the M/V *Kennicott* struck rocks at Light 39 just north of Green Rocks. Too much Becker rudder angle was used to make the turn to port at Green Rocks. With Becker rudders, the *Kennicott* turns quickly, and the master could not recover in time to prevent striking the rocks at Light 39 and puncturing a hole in the ship's bulbous bow.
- On a strong flood current, some have advised that it may be helpful to turn at Buoy 60 toward the harbor and maneuver into the back eddies, being mindful of speed and control. However, *this can be a risky maneuver.* It is noteworthy that when pilots for the Southeast Alaska Pilot Association guide small Japanese cargo ships to these cannery docks, they do so only at slack water. On May 7, 2012, during a strong flood current, the southbound M/V *Matanuska* was maneuvering into the back eddies inside of Buoy 60. With her stern extending out into the main current stream, the ship began

129 Captain Alan Doty, personal communication, 1999.

> to spin sharply to port. Fighting for control, the ship's master tried bringing the ship around to the starboard, all the while advancing toward the Ocean Beauty Seafood cannery dock, striking the dock nearly perpendicularly with her bow, and causing much damage to the cannery dock and buildings.

A pilotage applicant must reproduce all chartlets of Wrangell Narrows from memory and write an extensive route description after documenting a required number of round-trip passages. The applicant must also describe all the aids to navigation verbatim as published in the *Light List*. The 22.5-nautical-mile waterway is separated into five examination chartlets to draw. A partial understanding comes from oral accounts, reading, and study. Much geographic and navigational detail must be absorbed and committed to memory.

The pilotage examination is a rite of passage. Its purpose is to enhance local knowledge. The pilotage applicant should listen carefully to those with experience in Wrangell Narrows. A more complete understanding comes after making many trips through the narrows and observing these transits both northbound and southbound, in all weathers and times of the day or night, with different masters and pilots. Such is the portfolio of a senior master or pilot with the Alaska Marine Highway System, who has made many hundreds to several thousand round-trip passages. Wrangell Narrows reveals its secrets slowly to attentive observers.

Success in safe navigation through this waterway requires an investment of patience and practice. Captain Payne demonstrated this with a pair of binoculars. Pointing to the right monocular and then to the left monocular, he said, "This is the right side of the channel, and this is the left side of the channel. In between is the middle of the channel. Some men know where the middle is, and some men do not," adding, "practice until Wrangell Narrows becomes an intimate friend."

Acquiring the knowledge of the waterway and the experience of how to handle the ship are paramount. Disaster lurks just outside the wheelhouse window. Whether a navigator is an old veteran or new to Wrangell Narrows, this waterway is no place for sentimentality. Knowledge of the channel and a vessel's behavior within it is slowly acquired. Both ingredients are essential for mastery of this channel.

A well-done job conning and handling a ship through Wrangell Narrows awards great satisfaction to any mariner.

NOAA Nautical Chart 17325: Wrangell Narrows

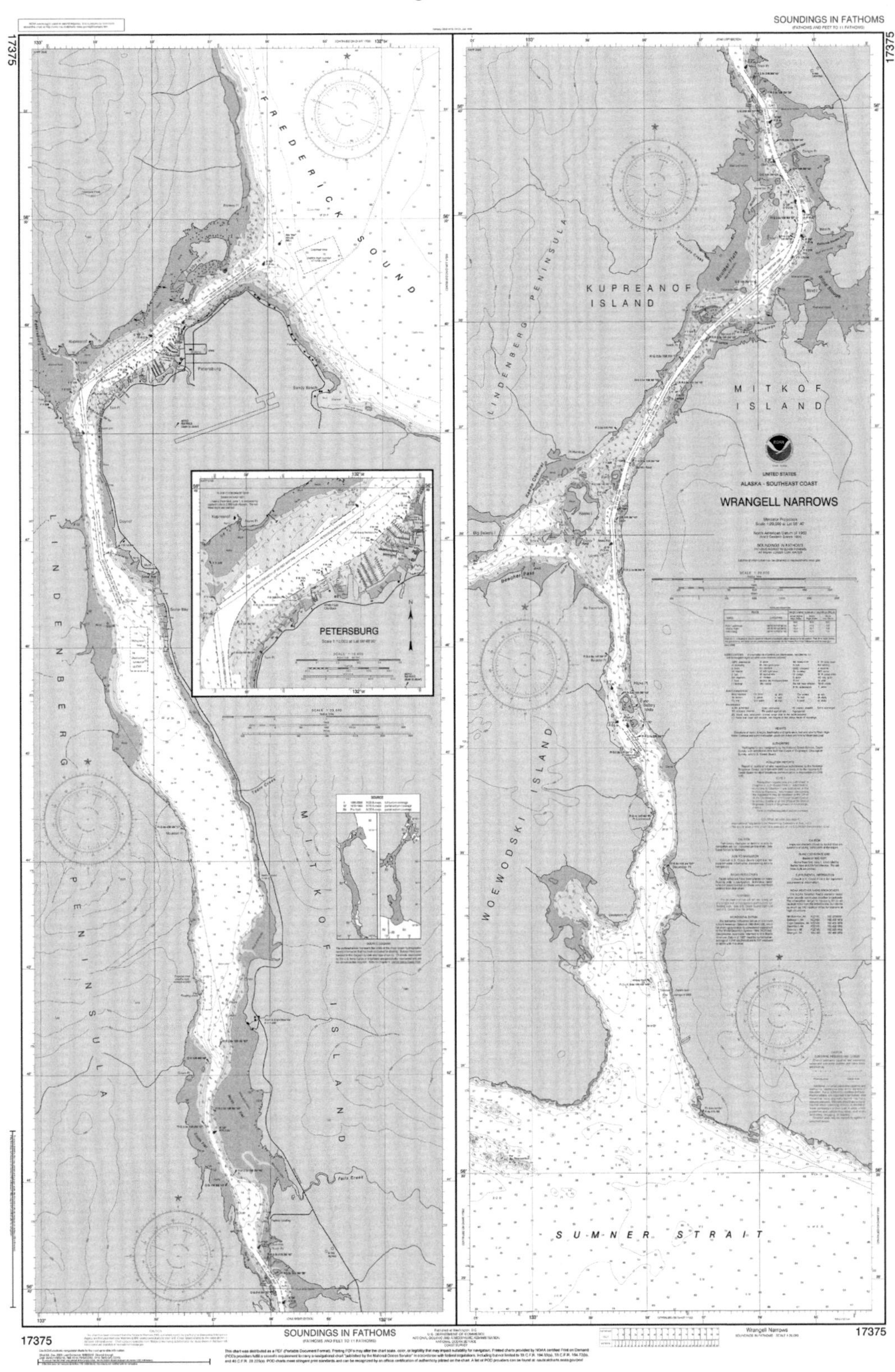

Wrangell Narrows

General

General

Securité Calls on VHF Channels 13 and 16

- When coming from Wrangell or Stikine Strait, give a Securité call at Station Island. VHF transmissions are heard and received from Station Island to and from vessels in Wrangell Narrows.
- Give a second Securité call at Point Alexander to be in communication with vessels transiting Wrangell Narrows.
- If entering Wrangell Narrows from the north, give a Securité call 10 to 20 minutes before Buoy WN at Sukoi Islands.
- Give a second Securité call at Mountain Point to be in communication with other vessels transiting Wrangell Narrows.
- Give a Securité call before departing Petersburg southbound or northbound.
- Securité calls should be in the full-power mode instead of 1 watt so that the radio signal can reach through the entire length of the narrows.
- A vessel that has given a Securité call and is of concern should be answered. Remember: Concerned traffic is traffic that can report visibility, ice, and traffic conditions, even though this traffic may not meet your vessel directly.

Radar Range Scales

- For navigating Wrangell Narrows, the ¾-mile range is best for clarity and visibility to the next course change.

- It is most advantageous to have the sweep at the center of the scope so that the outer scale can be used as a quick reference to determine either a bearing or the next course to steer. Offsetting the picture requires the observer to focus attention on a set of numbers in a field box, which is away from the picture when using an EBL.
- In this case, it is useless to use a mechanical cursor with the offset picture because the outer scale cannot be utilized.
- If necessary, the scale should be switched to the 1½-mile range to look ahead.
- Individual preferences govern choice of radar orientation. On AMHS vessels, the *Relative Stabilized North Up* presentation is frequently used. This stabilizes the picture while instantly showing the trails of vessels that are under way, making it easy to distinguish an aid to navigation from a moving vessel. North is always at the top of the screen, and the heading flash moves to indicate the vessel's true heading. Some masters prefer the *Relative Unstabilized Ship's Head Up* presentation. This gives the relative view seen from the wheelhouse windows; however, the picture and targets move when the course is changed. In this view, the ship's heading is continually at the top of the screen and does not move.

Maxims

- Have the most competent helmsman steer through Wrangell Narrows.
- Adjust and tune radars for maximum clarity of picture, with rain and sea clutter either turned down to a minimum or turned off.
- Have anchors ready for immediate release, and post a lookout on the bow.

- The engines should be on standby and ready for immediate maneuver.
- Instruct mates to speak out immediately if something does not look right.
- Teamwork is essential in fog or heavy snow. One mate should watch the radars and listen to the captain's conning orders in case of an error. Another mate should verify that conning orders are carried out, respond to the VHF radio, and fill in the logbook.
- Filling in a logbook is of secondary importance to safe navigation of the vessel.
- Be vigilant at the north end of Wrangell Narrows, from Light 50 to Buoy WN, and beyond to Cape Strait. Anticipate the possibility of encountering icebergs that calve from Le Conte Glacier.
- Have a searchlight with a strong beam of light ready for use.
- Either a fathometer or recording fathometer should be turned on.
- The VHF radios should be monitoring channels 13 and 16. Squelch should be properly adjusted to minimize static noise.
- When lined up on a range, the course may be compared with the actual range direction. The difference is a vessel's compass error.

Limitations

- On vessels of the Alaska Marine Highway System, the in-house rule is to enter Wrangell Narrows on a two-foot tidal holdover and greater. Exceptions are the M/V *Columbia* and the M/V *Kennicott*, which use four- and five-foot holdovers, respectively.

- Entering Wrangell Narrows in the fog is at the discretion of the individual master.
- In good visibility, it is prudent to measure distances both from points of land and from objects abeam of the ship. Distance measurements should also be taken when initiating a turn or navigating on a range. When committed to memory, these measurements provide a level of confidence in reduced visibility.
- A vessel can experience bank cushion, bank suction, and squatting due to shallow water. In this event, reduce speed to retain firm control of the vessel.
- Using buoys for reference, course changes, and headings can be unreliable.

Currents

- The tidal currents in Wrangell Narrows enter from both the northern and southern entrances, meeting and separating at Green Point. Green Point should not be confused with Green Rocks.
- Areas of strongest current occur at the following places:
  - The northern entrance to Turn Point
  - The reach between Light 18—North Ledge and Light 16—South Ledge
  - The reaches between Burnt Island and Spike Rock
  - The reaches around the Battery Islets
- For a vessel not on a schedule, it is advantageous to time the entrance to Wrangell Narrows in order to ride the flood current to the time of high-water slack at Green Point. The ebb current can be ridden the rest of the way. Some masters prefer to enter Wrangell Narrows at the end of or late on the flood tide when water depth is greatest.

- Another school of thought says that a ship steers more easily going with the current, which is correct. Additionally, in the event of engine failure or if it becomes necessary to stop, stemming the current allows the vessel to be slowed or anchored without the danger of the ship swinging around with the current.
- The strength of the current at its maximum can be between four and five knots, except during spring tides, when these currents can increase to six and seven knots.
- Table 2, Current Differences and Other Constants, found in the *Tidal Current Tables*, provides the Spike Rock and South Ledge current speed ratios for both ebb and flood currents. They are 1.2 times stronger than the current found off Petersburg.
- There is a strong westerly set, especially around the vicinity of Prolewy Rocks. At the end of the flood and the first of the ebb, an unexpected current sets northwest directly across the channel.

Charts and Publications

- *US Coast Pilot 8* is a good description of Wrangell Narrows. It is wise to study it in detail.
- Keep the nautical charts, *Coast Pilot 8*, and the *Light List* corrected to the most recent edition of the *Local Notices to Mariners*.
- Wrangell Narrows is depicted on NOAA *Nautical Chart 17375*. Only use the latest edition.
- *The Navigation Rules—International and Inland*, known as the Nautical Rules of the Road, is a valuable reference. Pay particular attention to Rule 9 concerning narrow channels, Rule 13 overtaking other vessels, Rule 19 conduct of vessels

in restricted visibility, and Rule 35 sound signals in restricted visibility.

General Interest

- Wrangell Narrows is 22.3 nautical miles in length.
- There are 26 course changes along the route.
- There are 71 aids to navigation for the main channel, excluding dock lights.
- There are five aids to navigation for the tow channel:
    - Papke's Landing: locality, on the west coast of Mitkof Island, nine miles south of Petersburg. This is a local name recorded in 1953 by the USGS. Named for early settler Dutch Papke.
    - Tonka: locality, on the Kupreanof Island shore south of Mountain Point and just north of Tonka Landing. This was the site of a cannery built in 1901 and relocated to Petersburg in 1906. It is said that the Kildahl brothers, who established the well-known Kildahl navigation school in Seattle, were raised here.
    - Doyhof: settlement on the west coast of Mitkof Island, one mile south of Petersburg. Former cannery, the name of which was derived from the last names of Meyer Hofstad and his partner, Doyan. The Doyhof post office was established in 1918 and discontinued in 1936.
    - Scow Bay: originally a local name used by fishermen and noted in 1912. The Scow Bay neighborhood is a suburb of Petersburg and was a part of Doyhof.
    - Kupreanof: settlement west of Petersburg on the Kupreanof Island coast at the northern entrance to Wrangell Narrows.

- Petersburg: town on the north end of Mitkof Island at the north entrance to Wrangell Narrows. Known as Little Norway, the town is largely inhabited by people of Scandinavian descent. The town grew up around a salmon cannery and sawmill built in 1897–1899 by Peter Buschmann, after whom it is named. The post office was established in 1900.

Channel Depths

- A federal project depth is the design dredging depth of a channel. The federal project depth provides for dredged sections that are 24 feet except for the dredged section west of Turn Point, which has a project depth of 27 feet.
- For controlling depths, consult regularly with *Local Notices to Mariners*. The controlling depth is less than federal project depths because of silting. Channel cuts have a tendency to fill, resulting in the need for considerable maintenance dredging. The controlling depth is the least depth in the channel governing the maximum draft of a vessel entering the narrows.
- Extreme high barometric pressure can also cause tides to be unpredictably lower than tabulated.
- Several times a year, exceptionally large spring tides occur and the water level may fall as much as four feet below the chart datum.
- The roadstead or anchorage area between Light 21 and Light 25 at Blind Slough has a federal project depth of 26 feet.

Weather

- Wrangell Narrows is generally shielded from the high winds that can occur in the main channels of Southeastern Alaska.

- According to the *Coast Pilot*, fog is observed on an average of 10 to 12 days per month except September and October, when fog occurs an average of 16 to 19 days each month.
- Heavy snowfall is the greatest restrictor of visibility in the winter, as snow accumulation covers many navigational lights from view.
- Fog is most likely during the early-morning hours, especially at Blind Slough.
- During times of high southeastern winds, forceful winds can blow through the valley on Mitkof Island opposite from Tonka Landing. These winds fan out to the north to Light 52.
- Call the Juneau National Weather Service 24-hour desk at 907-790-6800 for current weather conditions and forecasts.

Regulations

- A speed limit of seven knots is prescribed for Wrangell Narrows off Petersburg Harbor.
- No craft or tow shall be anchored in Wrangell Narrows in either the main ship channel or the towing channel, nor shall any craft or tow be anchored so that it can swing into either of these channels.
- Disabled craft in a condition of absolute necessity are exempt from the regulations.
- For details on Wrangell Narrows regulations, refer to *US Coast Pilot 8*, Chapter 2, part 162.255.

Commercial and Sport Fishing

- Shrimp beam trawling: Usually takes place near Point Alexander and Midway Rock. Seasons are May 1–June 30, July 1–August 31, and September 1–February 14.

- Pot shrimp fishing: Found in the southern end of Wrangell Narrows near Point Alexander and Midway Rock. The season is held October 1–February 28.
- Dungeness crab: Seasons runs June 15–August 15 and October 1–November 30. Most Dungeness crab gear is found between Light 50 and Light 52 in Scow Bay.
- King crab: Includes both male red and brown king crab. Red king crab season runs November 1–January 24. Brown king crab season runs from February 15 until the quota is filled. These fisheries are located at the southern entrance to Wrangell Narrows.
- Tanner crab: Season runs February 15–May 1. The fishery is usually located at the southern entrance to Wrangell Narrows.
- Herring: There is no herring fishery in Wrangell Narrows.
- Salmon troll: Winter fishery runs October 1–April 14, and the summer fishery April 15–September 30.
- King salmon troll: Winter fishery runs October 11–April 14, spring fishery is April 15–June 30, and summer fishery is July 1–September 30.
- Coho salmon troll: Runs June 15–September 20.
- Salmon purse seine fishery: Established by emergency order only.
- Salmon gillnet fishery: Established by emergency order only.
- Wrangell Narrows–Blind Slough Terminal Harvest Area: Established by emergency order, for the Crystal Lake Hatchery. The harvest is divided between commercial and sport fishers.
- Sportfishing: Sport salmon trolling occurs throughout the summer months.

Range Bearings and Reciprocals

- Petersburg Bar Range 235.5/055.5 degrees
- Petersburg Creek Range 353.2/173.2 degrees
- Blind Slough Range 050.3/230.3 degrees
- Bush Top Island Range 029.0/209.0 degrees
- Burnt Island Range 356.5/176.5 degrees

Hydrographic Surveys

- Detailed hydrographic surveys of Wrangell Narrows can be obtained from the Army Corps of Engineers. Write to:

  Alaska District Office
  Army Corps of Engineers
  Bldg. 21-700
  Elmendorf Air Force Base
  Box 898
  Anchorage, AK 99506-0898

General Precautions

- It is usually easier to begin a turn early and check the vessel's swing than it is to turn late and depart the channel.
- For most turns, when and how much rudder to use depends largely on the strength and direction of the current, and whether the ship is stemming the current or traveling with the current.
- When overtaking another vessel in the narrows, the vessel being overtaken has the right of way. If possible, reduce speed early enough so that the vessel ahead can be overtaken at a safe location. If this is not practicable, make arrangements via the VHF radio to overtake where the channel widens at Petersburg, Scow Bay, Papke's Landing, or between Light 21 and Light 25.

- In the summer months, anticipate recreational boating traffic in the form of both yachts and sport fishers. Sometimes such boaters do not pay attention to the presence of larger craft.
- When meeting another vessel in the narrows, arrange for one vessel to wait outside the narrows until the other vessel clears. If this is not practicable, make mutual agreement on VHF radio to meet at a wide portion of the channel. Coordinate speeds in order to pass at one of the locations mentioned above. Frequent communication, with the meeting vessel updating its position, is important for the sake of safe passage.
- Current velocity, water depth, and vessel handling characteristics determine the maximum speed that the ship can safely travel. It is vital to be aware of the ship's wake, especially when entering from the north, Scow Bay, Tonka, Papke's Landing, and the resorts near Green Rocks.
- If a slower vessel ahead offers to pull aside, do not discourage it. It is best for the faster vessel to pass the slower vessel and have it fall in behind at the earliest opportunity.
- A ship pilot should never be pressured into taking an unnecessary risk. Do not underestimate the value of common sense.
- Keep pilothouse chatter to a minimum. Maintain concentration.

What follows are northbound and southbound route descriptions for Wrangell Narrows. These are for general interest only.

Wrangell Narrows Course Card

NORTHBOUND

Course Change Locations	*True Compass Courses*
Point Alexander.	350
Midway Rock	010
Point Lockwood	343
Lockwood Rock	322
Buoy #2A	346
Light #4 Battery Islets	010
Boulder Point	356 Range
Light #10	017
Light #14	029 Range
Light #16 South Ledge	037
Light #18 North Ledge	050 Range
Light #21 Colorado Reef	041
Light #25	015
Buoy #29	333
Light #32A	348
Green Rocks Light #37	327
Buoy #42	350
Finger Point.	335
Buoy #46	352
Light #48	008
Light #49	000
Mountain Point Light.	337
Light #52	353 Range
Turn Point	055 Range
Buoy #63 (WN)	342

Run 60 to 75 seconds past "WN" before turning

Wrangell Narrows Course Card

SOUTHBOUND

Course Change Locations	*True Compass Courses*
Buoy #63 (WN)	235 Range
Turn Point	174 Range
Light #52	157
Mountain Point Light	180
Light #50	188
Light #48	172
Buoy #46	155
Finger Point.	167
Buoy #42	148
Green Rocks Light #37	170
Light #32A	151
Buoy #29	174
Light #25	217
Light #21 Colorado Reef	230 Range
Light #l8 North Ledge	217
Light #16 South Ledge	209 Range
Light #14	197
Light #10	176 Range
Boulder Point	190
Light #4 Battery Islets	165
Buoy #2A	142
Lockwood Rock	162
Point Lockwood	190
Midway Rock.	175
Point Alexander.	104

Distance Chart

Wrangell Narrows

	Point Alexander	Midway Island	Point Lockwood	Battery Islets	Burnt Island	Bush Top Island	Blind Point	Green Rocks	Papke's Landing	Green Point	Mountain Point	Blunt Point	Turn Point	Dock Petersburg
Midway Island	1.9													
Point Lockwood	3.5	1.6												
Battery Islets	4.7	2.8	1.2											
Burnt Island	6.9	5	3.4	2.2										
Bush Top Island	8.6	6.7	5.1	3.9	1.7									
Blind Point	9.8	7.9	6.3	5.1	2.9	1.2								
Green Rocks	11.1	9.2	7.6	6.4	4.2	2.5	1.3							
Papke's Landing	11.6	9.7	8.1	6.9	4.7	3.0	1.8	0.5						
Green Point	13.1	11.2	9.6	8.4	6.2	4.5	3.3	2.0	1.5					
Mountain Point	15.4	13.5	11.9	10.7	8.5	6.8	5.6	4.3	3.8	2.3				
Blunt Point	18.0	16.1	14.5	13.3	11.1	9.4	8.2	6.9	6.4	4.9	2.6			
Turn Point	19.6	17.7	16.1	14.9	12.7	11.0	9.8	8.5	8.0	6.5	4.2	1.6		
Dock Petersburg	20.3	18.4	16.8	15.6	13.4	11.7	10.5	9.2	8.7	7.2	4.9	2.3	0.7	
Buoy "WN"	22.3	20.4	18.8	17.6	15.4	13.7	12.5	11.2	10.7	9.2	6.9	4.3	2.7	2.0

Wrangell Narrows

Northbound Passage

Northbound Passage

1. **Point Alexander Light, the southern entrance into Wrangell Narrows:** When coming from Vichnefski Rock steering 030 degrees true on the Point Alexander Light, set the VRM (variable range marker) to 0.70 NM (nautical miles). Wait for the VRM to touch Point Alexander dead ahead, and then come to the port to a course of 350 degrees true. The ship will be heading on Deception Point to be 0.15 NM off Midway Rock Light on the starboard side. The radar's index line or EBL (electronic bearing line) could also be used to determine when to make this course change.

   When coming from Wrangell or Stikine Strait and heading on Foremost Rock Daybeacon, on a course of 283 degrees true, set the VRM to 0.45 NM and alter course so that Point Alexander Light will be 0.45 NM when abeam. A navigator can use the radar index line to determine this course if necessary. When Point Alexander is abeam at 0.45 NM, adjust the rate of turn to keep the light constantly on the beam at this distance. Allow the helmsman at least 10 degrees notice to steady on a course of 350 degrees true. Point Alexander Light should be abeam at 0.45 NM with the vessel lined up to be 0.15 NM off Midway Rock. A less precise method is to come abeam of Point Alexander Light while steering on Foremost Rock on a course of 283 degrees true and swing gently to the starboard, 0.60 NM distance off at the beginning of the turn, 0.40 NM distance off at the end of the turn. Steady up on course 350 degrees true, heading on the right-hand nub of Deception Point in order to be 0.15 NM off Midway Rock Light.

Note: Give a Securité call before initiating the turn to determine whether there is channel-blocking traffic in the narrows. If so, wait in the open waters of eastern Sumner Strait for the traffic to clear the channel. Make sure that the engines are on standby, the master has been called, a bow lookout has been posted, and the anchor or anchors are cleared and ready for immediate let go.

Note: Be aware of the shoal water off Woewodski Island on the west side of the entrance between Point Alexander and Midway Rock.

2. **Midway Rock Light MR:** Turn when abeam or a little before abeam to the starboard, steadying up on a course of 010 degrees true to pass midchannel between December Point and Point Lockwood. Begin to slow down to a comfortable speed for steerage and currents, but never at full speed. Keep a little extra speed and power in reserve if needed for a critical moment.

   Note: During the summer months, gillnet fishing vessels will raft alongside fish packers in the bight between December Point and Midway Rock to deliver their catch. Commercial fishing vessels also use this area for anchorage. Others may anchor just south of Deception Point.

   Note: On the flood, between Deception Point and Point Lockwood, there is a strong tendency to set to the west.

   Note: Captain Jeff Baken of the Southeast Alaska Pilots Association advises, "If required to wait for fog (or for a pilot) a good anchorage can be found at 56° 32.09′ N and 132° 58.59′ W on the north end of a four-fathom bank, in five fathoms of water with a mud and shale bottom. This is a temporary anchorage as it is exposed to SE winds."[130]

130 Captain Jeff Baken, email correspondence, January 2, 2019.

3. **Point Lockwood Light PL:** Turn to the port when Point Lockwood Light "PL" is on the port bow or when the EBL is set to 343 degrees true and splits Lockwood Rock 1 and Light 2 at 0.08 to 0.10 NM distance off Point Lockwood. Come to a course of 342–343 degrees true, heading on the east tangent of the Battery Islets. Boulder Point, Light 2, and Battery Island should all be in a line at the end of this turn. Set the variable range ring on the radar to 0.22 NM.

4. **Lockwood Rock Light 1, Battery Islets:** When VRM set to 0.22 NM touches Lockwood Rock Light 1, begin changing the course to port. Change the course and steady up on course 322 degrees true to pass midchannel, heading on a small indentation in the Woewodski Island shoreline ahead.

   Visually, when Buoy 3 is slightly open to the right of Lockwood Rock Light, it is time to begin changing the course. Another method is to set the EBL to 323 degrees true, and when the EBL lines up on Lockwood Rock change the course. Light 4A and Little Battery Islet should line up at the end of the turn. Light 2 is 30 feet outside the channel.

   Note: If the course change is made too late, the ship will be too close to Light 2. If the course change is made too soon, the ship will be too close to Lockwood Rock.

   Note: Currents can be strong when rounding the Battery Islets. This heading should bisect the channel. Be aware of setting to the west on both the flood and the ebb tides.

   Note: A ledge extends southeast of Light 2 along the side of the channel on the starboard side.

5. **Buoy 2A:** On smaller vessels, come abeam of Buoy 2A. Larger vessels should begin this turn 0.08 NM prior and turn with moderate rudder to the starboard, steadying up on a course of 348 degrees true with Buoy 5 showing slightly to the port ahead. The heading should fall between Buoy 5 and the Boulder Point Light 7 when looking ahead. Be aware of the ledge off the west side of

the Battery Islets. Another method is to set the EBL to 348 degrees true. When it lines up on Light 4A, start the turn. Keene Island and No Thorofare Point should not close.

6. **Light 4A:** On smaller vessels, come abeam of Light 4A. On larger vessels, turn to the starboard when the VRM set to 0.08 NM touches Light 4A. Use a moderate amount of rudder and steady up on a course of 010 degrees true. Favor the Woewodski Island side of the channel when passing between Buoy 5 and Light 4A to remain clear of the three-fathom ledge north of Light 4A. It is not good to be right-handed or tight on Light 4A. If visibility permits, look ahead to the Burnt Island Range. Gauge the next turn to the port at Boulder Point Light 7 accordingly to be on the Burnt Island Range. Light 4A stands 90 feet outside the channel limit.

7. **Boulder Point Light 7, Burnt Island Range, and Spike Rock:** Turn to the port with an easy-to-moderate swing when the time is right to be on the Burnt Island Range 356 degrees true. If visibility is limited, turn when abeam of Boulder Point Light 7 or slightly past abeam. Many have a tendency to turn a little too early or too quickly. Adjust the course to be 0.08 NM off No Thorofare Point when on the range and clear of Spike Rock. Spike Rock Buoy 9 is set inside the channel limit. It is acceptable to stay slightly to the right in order to keep away from Spike Rock. Smaller vessels can pull over just north of No Thorofare Point to stay clear of larger vessels. Also, when the EBL has been set to 356 degrees true and lines up on Spike Rock Buoy 9, begin the turn (if the buoy is in its proper position).

   Note: Spike Rock is close to the western edge of the channel. Uncharted pinnacles in the area of Spike Rock have been reported. It is important to be on the Burnt Island Range or slightly right-handed when passing Spike Rock northbound.

   Note: On the reach between Boulder Point and Light 10 there is a tidal set due to the currents to and from Beecher Pass. The current sets to the right on the ebb and to the left set on the flood. Correct the course accordingly to stay on the Burnt Island Range ahead.

8. **Light 10:** On smaller vessels come abeam of Light 10, and on larger vessels 0.08 NM prior. Turn to the starboard smartly to steady up on a course of 017 degrees true and pass midchannel between Buoy 13A and Light 14. Have the EBL bearing 016 degrees true, and begin the turn when it lines up on Light 14. This is a critical course change. If the ship turns too soon, it will be too close to the foul area behind Daybeacon 10A. If the ship turns too late, it will be too close to Burnt Island. Stay midchannel and never overtake another vessel here. Light 10 is 30 feet outside the channel limit.

9. **Light 14, Burnt Reef:** Gauge the turn accordingly to be on the Bush Top Range. Come abeam of Light 14 on smaller vessels and 0.08 NM prior on larger vessels. Turn to the starboard and steady up on a course of 029 degrees true on the range. Another method is to have the EBL set to 029 degrees true and begin the turn when the EBL splits Light 16 and Light 17. Be aware of a rapid set from Keene Channel. The tidal currents set to the left on the ebb and to the right on a flood. Set is predominantly, but not always, to the left on an ebb tide. Adjust the course to stay on the range. Notice that when on this range Light 17 is slightly on the starboard side ahead. There is sufficient room for a vessel to pull out of the channel to await traffic just south of Light 15. It can be difficult to hold position in the current, however. Light 14 is 30 feet outside the channel limit.

10. **Light 15 and Light 16, South Ledge:** Midway between Light 15 and Light 16, begin the turn to the starboard, steadying up on a course of 037 degrees true to pass Light 17 on the port side. The heading should split Light 17 and Light 18. Observe the current on the piling of Light 17 to see its strength. The reach between Light 16—South Ledge and Light 18—North Ledge has the strongest current in Wrangell Narrows. The current ratio is 1.2 time stronger than at Turn Point. Awareness of a vessel's wake is critical

due to the large number of property owners along the shoreline. However, adequate power is necessary for control and steerage of the ship. Light 16 is 30 feet outside the channel limit.

11. **Light 18, North Ledge:** Turn to the starboard. Gauge the turn by observing the Blind Slough Range ahead, and steady up on a course of 050 degrees true to be on the range. Keep well away from Light 18, which stands nearly 100 feet outside the channel limit. If the Blind Slough Range is not visible, change course to 050 degrees true when Light 18—North Ledge is abeam or slightly prior and pass midway between Spruce Point and Light 19.

12. **Light 21, Colorado Reef:** Change course to the port when abeam or just prior to be heading on Buoy R26 on a course of 041 degrees true. A navigator may also start the turn when the EBL, set to 040, lines up between Light 25 and Buoy R26. Set the VRM on the radar to 0.15 NM. Light 21 is 30 feet outside the channel limit.

    Note: Be aware of a submerged 16-foot rock on the starboard side at the channel limit opposite Light 21.

    Note: The dredged area between Light 21—Colorado Reef and Light 25 is a safe refuge to await northbound and southbound traffic. The VHF radio and the six-minute rule (a vessel travels one-tenth of its speed in six minutes, six minutes being the tenth part of an hour) are helpful tools in determining what speed is needed to arrive at the dredged area to meet with opposing traffic. For example, a vessel traveling at 11.0 knots will advance 1.10 NM in six minutes. When alerted to the presence of another large vessel on the radio, the opposing vessel's position and speed can be ascertained. By using the six-minute rule and stepping out the opposing traffic's intended track with a set of dividers, its ETA (estimated time of arrival) to the dredged area can be determined. It is then possible to adjust the vessel's speed to have the same ETA as the opposing craft. Make periodic calls on the VHF to monitor the opposing vessel's progress. Adjust the speed to maintain the same ETA so that the vessels will meet precisely between Light 25 and Light 21 at Colorado Reef.

Note: Blind Slough Front Range Light is 40 feet outside the channel limit, and Light 25 is 30 feet outside the channel limit. Buoy R26 is 30 feet outside the channel limit.

13. **Light 25, Blind Slough:** When the 0.15 NM variable range ring touches Light 25, it is time to begin the turn to port, or nearly so, depending upon the vessel. Enough rudder angle should be used to begin turning to the port and steadying up on an intermediate course of 015 degrees true. Sometimes this turn is accomplished without steadying up on an intermediate course, depending upon tidal currents and the vessel's rate of turn. The variable range ring on the radar should remain set at 0.15 NM. Stay midchannel passing Light 27, which is 90 feet outside the channel limit. Caution: It is easy to overrun this turn and end up on top of Buoy R26. The EBL, bearing 015 degrees true, should point at Buoy 28 during the swing.

14. **Buoy 29:** When passing Light 27 or when the 0.15 NM variable range ring touches Buoy 29, resume the turn to port as conditions dictate. Steady up on a course of 333 degrees true when rounding Buoy 29 to pass midchannel between Buoy 33 and Light 32A. The heading should be on the right tangent of Island Point ahead. It is reasonable to be a little left-handed on this reach due to Lights 32 and 32A being set outside the channel limit. Buoy 29 is 15 feet outside the channel limit, and Light 32 is 60 feet outside the channel limit. Light 32A is 30 feet outside the channel limit. Light 32 and Green Rocks should not open.

15. **Light 32A:** Turn to starboard when Light 32A is abeam. Steady up on a course of 348 degrees true steering tangent to Rock Point ahead with the beautiful log homes. Light 37 and Light 40 line up after the turn is completed. Another method is to set the EBL to 347 degrees true. When the EBL touches Buoy 36, begin the

turn. Do not confuse Light 34 with Light 32A. If a turn is made at Light 34, it is too late. This course is critical to prepare for the next course change at Light 37—Green Rocks. Buoy 33 is 30 feet outside the channel limit, and Light 34 is 60 feet outside the channel limit.

16. Light 37, Green Rocks: Turn to the port when Light 37 is on the port bow or just afterwards. The most reliable means of timing is the seaman's eye. The EBL can be set to 327 degrees true. When it touches Light 39, begin the turn. In reduced visibility, set the VRM to 0.08 NM. When Green Rocks passes a small distance inside the 0.08 NM variable range ring, begin changing course to the port.

The northbound turn is gentler than when southbound and generally requires a smaller amount of rudder because it begins from a different point of departure. However, a strong ebbing current may hold up the turn, and a strong flooding current may carry the ship too far to the starboard. If the vessel is tight on Green Rocks, the stern can be drawn toward Green Rocks, preventing the ship from turning to port. A vessel can actually "crab sideways" down the channel with the stern angled toward Green Rocks until the bank suction is released. Apply additional rudder to overcome this suction effect, as the speed should already be at a minimum. The suction effect is especially prevalent on a deep draft vessel with a broad beam.

Come to a course of 327 degrees true, remembering that Lights 38 and 40 stand 90 feet outside the channel limit. Although at times difficult to see, Light 38 and Light 48 should not open. Steady up on a course of 327 degrees true and begin slowing down. The fishing lodges on the Kupreanof Island shore behind Green Rocks request that ships maintain a minimum-wake speed while passing their docks, especially during the summer. In doing so, a navigator needs to monitor any set from the current, especially with an ebbing current when a ship can be set toward Buoy 36 and the foul area southeast of Green Rocks. Slow down to a no-wake speed before Papke's Landing.

The M/V *Kennicott* approaching Green Rocks northbound in Wrangell Narrows. COURTESY OF CAPTAIN WILLIAM M. HOPKINS.

17. **Buoy 42, Papke's Landing:** Turn to starboard 0.08 NM before Buoy 42 and come to a course of 350 degrees true. This course heads on Light 50 and is tangent on Mountain Point beyond. The heading keeps the vessel farther off Finger Point on the port side. The lineup between Light 50 and Mountain Point can be seen at night and on the radar. As mentioned above, Papke's Landing must be passed at a no-wake speed. This is a good place to pull over for traffic.

18. **Finger Point, the Flats:** Turn to the port before the vessel is abeam of Finger Point. Visually, look beyond for Light 47 to be almost midway between Lights 43 and 44. On the radar, set up the cursor or EBL for a course of 335 degrees true and turn when judgment

says the vessel will come out on course near 335 degrees true to pass midway between Lights 43 and 44. The turn can begin when Light 44 is 0.40 NM ahead. When on a course of 335 degrees true, steer nearly on Light 47 ahead and pass safely through the Flats. Between the Flats is found a deeper part of the channel. Light 44 and Light 48 line up when the ship points toward them during the turn.

19. **Buoy 46:** Come abeam of Buoy 46 or just prior and turn to the starboard. Steady up briefly on a course of 352 degrees true heading on the tangent of the point at Tonka Landing ahead. Another method is to set the EBL to 353 degrees true, and when it touches Light 48 begin the turn or 0.08 NM before Light 47. If possible, avoid meeting another vessel in this turn. There is not enough room to safely pass without a great amount of concentration, cooperation, and good communication.

    Note: Tidal currents meet and separate in the area of Green Point. Any currents are weak.

20. **Light 48:** Turn to starboard when Light 48 is on the starboard bow or slightly after. Steady up on course 008 degrees true. Place Light 47 dead astern and line up between Light 49 and Light 50 ahead, two-thirds from Light 49 and one-third from Light 50. When the EBL is set to 008 degrees true and touches Light 50, begin the turn. Be aware of the shoal just above and below Light 48 on the starboard side of the channel. Light 50 is 30 feet outside the channel limit.

21. **Light 49:** When halfway between Light 49 and Light 50, begin the turn to the port and steady up on a course of 000 degrees true for Mountain Point. Stay well away from Light 49 on a lower tide. Slowly increase the speed to full ahead. Be aware, however, of any small boats that may be tied up at Tonka Landing.

22. **Mountain Point Light 51, Scow Bay:** Turn to port when the Mountain Point Light is slightly forward of the beam and come to a course of 337 degrees true. Slow down to a no-wake speed for Scow Bay when the vessel is abeam of the dock in front of the old Narrows Restaurant. Scow Bay is a good place to wait for traffic before continuing to Petersburg. The distance off Mountain Point should be 0.25 mile. The heading of 337 degrees should be just to the left of Light 52 ahead. Scow Bay is a good anchorage area.

    Note: Sometimes there is an unlighted mooring buoy to the east of Mountain Point toward the Mitkof Island shore. There may also be an unlighted barge secured to the buoy.

23. **Light 52:** Turn to the starboard and gauge the turn to be on the Petersburg Creek Range, steadying up on a course of 353 degrees true. A navigator may increase the speed to maintain control and steerage of the ship. Strong currents may be encountered at Turn Point. Be aware of set to right or left. Correct the course accordingly to remain on the range. Caution: At Light 52, watch for a set to the left on a strong flood current. Light 52 is 75 feet outside the channel limit. There can also be a strong set to the right near Buoy 53, just south of Turn Point, during a strong flood.

24. **Lights 54 through 58, Turn Point:** Come around Turn Point with a gradual swing to the starboard as necessary to stay in the channel. Vessels must slow down to a no-wake speed when passing Petersburg. This is a regulated speed zone of seven knots or less. More power may be needed as conditions demand for steerage and control of the ship. At Light 58 when continuing north, maneuver onto the Petersburg Bar Range astern. Steer 055 degrees true and adjust the course to remain on the Petersburg Bar Range until clear of Buoy WN, formerly called Buoy 63. Strong currents can be encountered in the last reach of Wrangell Narrows near the northern entrance to the narrows. A strong set to the northwest can occur on the last of the flood and the first of the ebb. On a

strong flood current, there is a set to the right toward Buoy 60. Lights 54, 56, and 58 are all 30 feet outside the channel limit.

Note: When going to the Petersburg Ferry Terminal, round Light 58 and steer on the Standard Oil Dock if the current is flooding. If the ebb is weak, go directly to the dock, starboard side to. If the ebb is stronger than 2.0 knots, it is wise to turn the vessel around and stem the ebb to the ferry terminal, landing port side to the dock. Regarding docking in the current at Petersburg, Captain Payne writes, "I like Petersburg at any strength of the current. The current can be used to a good advantage if used respectfully. Easy does it and no high ball operation here. The current can do most of the work for you."[131]

***Ship Handling—Destroyers* reminds us:** "When working your ship, always take into consideration the wind and the tide. Seldom are they not present. They are forces available to your hand as are your engines or your rudders. It is the smart ship handler who lets them work for him."[132]

Note: In summer 2005, a new shoal was discovered on the north end of Wrangell Narrows by the NOAA ship *Fairweather*. It is a mere 11 feet below the charted depth and just 70 feet outside the western edge of the north entrance channel limit. The position of the shoal is 56° 49′ 32.390″ N, 132° 56′ 26.450″ W, along the western edge of the north entrance channel and due north of the unnamed northernmost point of Mitkof Island, locally known as Hungry Point.

25. **Buoy WN (Whiskey November), Petersburg Bar:** This marks the exit into Frederick Sound. Once abeam of Buoy WN, use a watch or stopwatch to let 60 to 75 seconds elapse before changing course to the port and steadying up on course 342 degrees true for the Sukoi Islands. The turn may also be made 0.30 NM beyond Buoy WN. Another method is to set the VRM to 3.00 NM and begin the

131 Captain Harold Payne, personal communication, 1989.

132 Schmidt, *Ship Handling—Destroyers*, I-4.

turn just before McDonald Island in Frederick Sound contacts the 3.00 NM VRM circle. In reduced visibility, be 0.12 NM off Prolewy Rock to be in the center of the channel. Caution: Watch for set onto Buoy WN during a strong ebb current.

Note: Pronounced and vigorous tide rips with standing waves can be observed as water floods and ebbs over the Petersburg Bar at the northern entrance to Wrangell Narrows.

Note: When leaving Wrangell Narrows, be aware of icebergs that calve off Le Conte Glacier. These icebergs can sometimes be encountered inside Wrangell Narrows roughly as far as Light 50 and outside Wrangell Narrows as far as Cape Strait. They can be hard to detect by radar alone. A good searchlight is handy in Wrangell Narrows. A lightbulb is easier and less expensive to replace than sections of a steel hull!

Wrangell Narrows
Southbound Passage

Southbound Passage

Wrangell Narrows begins officially at Buoy WN, affectionately called Whiskey November. Certain preparations and precautions should be observed well before making the turn to enter the narrows and line up on the Petersburg Bar Range.

According to Captain Charles L. Bates:

> As early as Cape Strait, a navigator should begin scanning the water's surface for the presence of icebergs that calve off the Le Conte Glacier. Some larger pieces have been observed in recent times as far as a mile to the west of Cape Strait.
>
> Make sure the radar is finely tuned, properly using the minimum amount of sea clutter and the maximum amount of gain to detect icebergs. Long pulse also can be helpful in detecting these oftentimes low-lying growlers composed of hard blue ice, which, under the right circumstances, can penetrate the steel hull of a well-founded ship. It is important also to note the presence of any concentration of icebergs along the shore near the entrance to Thomas Bay. This will give an indication of how active the calving has been, alerting the navigator to the potential concentrations of ice. On rare occasions and at times of extreme high water and warm temperatures, the

ice concentration between Beacon Point and Buoy WN can be equivalent to the amount one would experience at the face of an active glacier. A steady course cannot be held as one is steering through the "open leads" or the widest path through the ice. The engines should be on standby and the vessel's speed slowed down enough to evaluate the alternatives and choose the best possible course. Often a "lead" will be circuitous requiring numerous course changes and rudder commands. Be suspect of every single radar target and aware that the "leads" observed are dynamic and open up and close with the wind and current. A "lead" can quickly disappear. A navigator must constantly appraise the situation and develop a strategy of continually searching and exploring alternatives for the best and safest course to take. Be especially vigilant at a tide line where icebergs can be entrapped.

While wending a ship through the maze do not forget the presence of traffic when entering into a busy fishing port at Petersburg. Often the intense focus of avoiding ice, especially at night or in reduced visibility, can distract the navigator from observing other vessels that are most likely steering an erratic course and focused upon ice avoidance as well. This is where an extra navigator on the bridge and a gentle reminder to the lookout can be of great value. A navigator should also have the VHF radio tuned to channels 13 and 16 to monitor any Securité calls. This will alert the navigator to the presence of potential traffic that may be encountered while approaching Buoy WN. The presence of traffic in the narrows may also indicate the action that must be taken to allow traffic to clear the narrows before you enter at Buoy WN.[133]

Note: Anchorage can be found on an underwater shoulder projecting northeastward from the unnamed point on the east side of the northern entrance to Wrangell Narrows in four to five fathoms, 0.28 NM from the shoreline. Be cautious of the sewer outfall to the south and consult the nautical chart. This unnamed point is the northernmost point of Mitkof Island and locally known in Petersburg as Hungry Point.

Note: Pronounced and vigorous tide rips with standing waves can be observed as water floods and ebbs over the Petersburg Bar at the northern entrance to Wrangell Narrows.

1. **Buoy WN (Whiskey November), the northern entrance into Wrangell Narrows:** When approaching the northern entrance into Wrangell Narrows from the northwest on a course of 162 degrees true, begin the entry turn when the Petersburg Bar Range becomes visible from behind Sasby Island or when Buoy WN is 63 degrees relative on the starboard bow. Other methods are to turn when Prolewy Rocks close visually with Sasby Island or to set the VRM to 1.10 NM. Begin the turn when the 1.10 NM variable range ring touches the unnamed point of land north of Petersburg at the entrance (Hungry Point). Regardless of the method used, steer on the Petersburg Bar Range at 235 degrees true. Place the ship on whatever heading is necessary to keep the range closed and in line. Be 0.12 NM off Prolewy Rocks on the starboard side. On the last of the flooding tide and during an ebbing tide, be aware of a strong set to the right or to the northwest when on the range. Begin to slow down to a no-wake speed for passing in front of Petersburg, being aware of the strength of the current at all times. This is a regulated speed zone of seven knots or less. More power may be needed as conditions demand for steerage and control of the ship.

133 Captain Charles L. Bates, personal notes.

Note: In summer 2005, a new shoal was discovered on the north end of Wrangell Narrows by the NOAA ship *Fairweather.* It was found a mere 11 feet below the charted depth and just 70 feet outside the western edge of the north entrance channel. The position of the shoal is 56° 49′ 32.390″ N, 132° 56′ 26.450″ W, along the western edge of the north entrance channel and due north of the unnamed northernmost point of Mitkof Island, locally known as Hungry Point.

2. **Buoy 60:** When heading into the Petersburg Ferry Terminal, steer a general course of 222 degrees true. If flooding strongly, steer on the Standard Oil Dock. If ebbing strongly, steer on the ferry terminal and stem the current while reducing speed. A flood current sets diagonally into the ferry terminal as it begins to round Turn Point. An approach to the ferry terminal should be made wide, keeping ample distance off the dock to allow the current to assist in setting the vessel into the berth. On a strong flood current, be careful that the ship does not set behind the ferry terminal dock before arriving there.

   Note: During a flood, a ship should depart from the dock by backing toward Buoy 59 in front of the Petersburg small boat harbor to avoid being set by the strong current onto Light 58. After completing the backing maneuver and when there is adequate sea room, return to the Petersburg Bar Range and resume the southbound passage.

3. **Lights 58 through 54, Turn Point:** This is a gradual midchannel turn. At Light 54, have the ship on the Petersburg Creek Range (353 degrees true) when looking astern. Steer 173 degrees true. Small course changes are needed to keep on the range due to the current buffeting the ship. This is an area of strong tidal current. Be aware of strong and rapid set toward Buoy 53 while making the turn, especially when the current is flooding from the north. Buoy 53 should not open with the shoreline west of Light 52. Observe Daybeacon 51A beyond Light 52. When these two aids come into

range with one another, they delineate the eastern limit of the channel between Light 54 and Light 52. If a vessel ends up beyond this range line, the ship is out of the channel.

Note: When looking astern at a range, the lower range board or light to the right or left of the after and higher range board or light will indicate if the ship is to the right or left of the range line. A navigator must correct the heading a degree or two accordingly. If the ship is to the right of the range line, it must come to the left. If the ship is to the left of the range line, it must come to the right.

4. **Light 52, Scow Bay:** Light 52 is 75 feet outside the channel limit. Change the course to 157 degrees true heading toward the bight at the south end of Scow Bay to be 0.25 NM off Mountain Point. Slow down to a no-wake speed for Scow Bay. You may increase speed when abeam of the dock in front of the old Narrows Restaurant.

   Note: If the tall twin radio towers at Papke's Landing are not visible, it may indicate fog in the narrows in the area of Blind Slough.

5. **Mountain Point Light 51:** Round easy and come to 181 degrees true. Place the heading one-third from Light 50 and two-thirds from Light 49.

   Note: Mountain Point is a good place to anchor up to wait for weather (fog) or for northbound traffic to clear the buoyed channel. Keep a sharp eye for the unlighted mooring buoy that is set near midstream off Mountain Point. This mooring buoy tends to move around. Sometimes there is an unlighted barge attached to it.

6. **Light 50, the Flats:** Slow down before arrival at Light 50 for narrows transit and the possibility of small vessels moored at Tonka Landing. Change the course halfway between Light 50 and Light 49 and steady up on a course of 188 degrees true heading on Light 47 with Light 50 astern. Stay clear of Light 49 at lower tides. Be aware of the shoaling area to the north and to the south

of Light 48 on the port side. Light 50 is 30 feet outside of the channel limit.

7. **Light 48:** Begin turning to the port before the ship is abeam of Light 48. Come to a course of 174 degrees true briefly or continue in a slow midchannel turn to Buoy 46. It is not advisable to meet with an oncoming vessel in this turn. Request the oncoming vessel to hold up at Papke's Landing.

8. **Buoy 46:** Turn to the port and steady up on a course of 155 degrees true on a heading midway between Light 44 and Light 43. This heading should either be nearly tangent to Rock Point ahead (the point with a beautiful log home) or on the middle of the shoal exposed in the distance just to the right when viewing Rock Point. The turn should be completed before Light 43 and Light 39 line up. At low water, this channel is one of the deeper areas and is well defined between the exposed mudflats.

   Note: Tidal currents meet and separate in the area of Green Point. Any currents are weak.

9. **Finger Point, Papke's Landing:** Begin the turn when the northern end of Finger Point is abeam on the starboard side. Come to a course of 167 degrees true and steer near the cabin immediately ahead and inside of the Green Rocks. Slow down to a no-wake speed for Papke's Landing. It is possible to pull over and wait for traffic. Buoy 42 and the trees on Green Rocks should line up during the turn.

10. **Buoy 42, Rock Point:** Begin the turn to the port when Light 38 lines up with Danger Point in the background. Buoy 42 should be forward of the port beam when beginning to change the course to the port. Another method is to set the VRM ring to 0.12 NM. Begin the turn when the 0.12 variable range ring touches Buoy 42. This is a moderate turn. Come to a course of 148 degrees true toward Danger Point. Increase the ship's speed for steerage and

Looking south in Wrangell Narrows from Papke's Landing showing the maze of lights and buoys that must be navigated. At night this is known as Pinball Alley. COURTESY OF CAPTAIN MATTHEW G. WILKENS.

control. This is necessary in order to make the next turn at Green Rocks, especially when stemming a large flood current. The fishing lodges on the Kupreanof shore behind Green Rocks request that ships maintain a minimum-wake speed when passing their docks during the summer. Lights 40 and 38 are 90 feet outside the channel limit. It is acceptable to be a little right-handed. Be aware of set onto Light 38 during a strong flood.

Note: Passing Green Rocks is similar to running a giant slalom course with a ship.

11. **Light 37, Green Rocks:** This is a critical turn, made with substantial rudder, especially when southbound against a flood current. It is made when Island Point breaks with Light 37 and no later. You can also begin this turn by setting the EBL to 170 degrees true and waiting for the EBL to clear with Green Rocks. If practicable,

the helm should be at midships before the turn, not in the opposite direction. Sometimes hard starboard rudder is necessary. Steady up on course 170–172 degrees true on the exposed rock off Vexation Point south of Buoy 33. The Blind Slough Front Range Light and the exposed rock should be in line. This rock is also visible on the radar most of the time. When passing Light 34, adjust the course slightly to 168 degrees true to make the next course change more gradual at Light 32A. Light 34 is 60 feet outside the channel limit.

12. **Light 32A:** Turn to the port when Buoy 33 is on the starboard bow and pass midchannel between Light 32A and Buoy 33. This is a gentle turn. Steady up on a course of 151 degrees true. The ship should be heading midway between the tangent to the point directly ahead and Buoy 28. Be aware of a strong set to the starboard during an ebbing current. It is permissible to be right-handed on this course, as Light 32A and Light 32 are set outside the channel limit. Light 33 is 30 feet outside the channel limit, and Light 32A is 30 feet outside the channel limit. Light 32 is 60 feet outside the channel limit.

13. **Buoy 29, Blind Slough:** Begin this turn to the starboard when Buoy 29 is on the starboard bow or when it is 0.08 NM ahead. Use discretion. This is usually a gentle turn, swinging to an intermediate course of 174 degrees true. The course heads nearly on the rear-range light of the Blind Slough Range. Continue with this turn to starboard when Light 27 is either on the bow or nearly so. Light 27 is 90 feet outside the channel limit. While in the turn passing Light 25, prepare to steady up on a course of 217 degrees true, heading on the tangent of Spruce Point or slightly inside this point to the left of the tangent. It is possible to pass on the back side (to the west) of Light 25 when meeting traffic in this turn. Although undesirable, it can be used with caution at higher tides. Light 29 is 15 feet outside the channel limit, and Buoy 26 is 30 feet outside the channel limit. Light 25 is 30 feet outside the channel

limit, and Blind Slough Front Range Light is 40 feet outside the channel limit.

14. **Light 21, Colorado Reef:** Turn just before Light 21 passes abeam. Steady up on a course of 230 degrees true, heading inside the small point just to the northwest of Light 15 and to the left of the left tangent of North Point. Adjust the course to stay on the Blind Slough Range astern. Pass midway between Light 19 and Spruce Point. Light 21 is 30 feet outside the channel limit.

    Note: Be aware of a submerged 16-foot rock on the port side at the channel limit opposite from Light 21.

15. **Light 18, North Ledge:** Turn to the port just before coming abeam of Light 18. Come to a course of 217 degrees true and head on the rear range light of the Burnt Island Range. Gauge this turn by observing the rear range light of the Burnt Island Range. When on a course of 217 degrees true, the Burnt Island after range light should be between Light 15 and Light 16 ahead. Light 18 stands nearly 100 feet outside the channel limit. Stay well away. Watch for set to the right on strong floods and ebbs. Light 17 and its tangent on the land should line up while swinging through this turn.

    Note: The reach between Light 18—North Ledge and Light 16—South Ledge is the area of strongest tidal current in Wrangell Narrows.

16. **Light 16, South Ledge:** Turn to the port and steady up initially on a course of 209 degrees true heading toward the left tangent of Burnt Island and between Buoy 13 and Buoy 13A. Check the Bush Top Range directly astern on this course. Adjust the course accordingly to remain on the range. Be aware of a rapid set from the tidal currents from Keene Channel that set to the right on the ebb and to the left on a flood. Set is predominantly, but not always, to the right on an ebb tide. The left tangent of Burnt Island and Keene Island can also be used as a range for this course. Light 16 is 30 feet outside the channel limit.

Note: It is possible to pull over just south of Light 15 outside the channel to await northbound traffic, though it is difficult to hold position in the current.

17. **Light 14, Burnt Reef:** Turn to the port when Buoy 13A is on the starboard bow 0.12 NM away. Another method is to set the VRM to 0.22 NM. Begin the turn when the 0.22 variable range ring touches the northern shore of Burnt Island ahead. Steady up on a course of 197–198 degrees true to pass Burnt Island on the starboard. Once past Light 11, ease the ship to the starboard to a course of 200 degrees true. This gives better clearance of the foul area marked by Daybeacon 10A. Light 14 and Buoy 13A are 30 feet outside the channel limit. The reach between Light 14 and Light 10 is an excellent area to see the effects of a vessel displacing water in a narrow channel, especially at low water.

18. **Light 10, Burnt Island Range, and Spike Rock:** This is a critical turn requiring considerable rudder. Start with a large amount of rudder (depending on the vessel). Begin the turn just before Light 8 and Light 10 line up in range with one another, or when Light 8 is in the middle of Battery Island ahead, or when Light 10 and Light 4A line up. The best method is to set the variable range ring on the radar to 0.14 NM. When this 0.14 NM range ring touches Light 10, it is time to begin the turn to port to 176 degrees true with a large amount of rudder (depending on the particular vessel). Do not confuse Daybeacon 10A with Light 10 beyond, which could cause the turn to be started too early. Steady on course 176 degrees true with the Burnt Island Range astern. Steady the heading on Light 4A and the right tangent of Battery Island. If the ship swings too wide on this turn, head on Light 8 to avoid being too close to Spike Rock Buoy 9. It is preferable to be left-handed when on the Burnt Island Range to avoid getting too close to Spike Rock Buoy 9, which is set just slightly inside the channel limit. Once past Spike Rock, adjust course to return to the Burnt Island Range. Smaller vessels can pull over and wait just north of No Thorofare Point for

traffic. Again, watch for any set to the starboard. Light 10 is 30 feet outside the channel limit.

Note: Spike Rock is close to the western edge of the channel. Uncharted pinnacles have been reported in the area of Spike Rock. It is important to be on the Burnt Island Range or slightly left-handed when passing Spike Rock southbound.

Note: On the reach between Light 10 and Boulder Point Light 7 there is a tidal set due to the currents to and from Beecher Pass. There is a left set on the ebb and a right set on the flood. Correct the course accordingly to stay on the Burnt Island Range astern.

19. **Boulder Point Light 7:** Turn when the light is forward of the starboard beam, or nearly so. A precise method is to set the VRM to 0.50 NM. When the 0.50 NM variable range ring touches the shoreline of the northernmost Battery Islet, change the course to 190 degrees true, heading for the bight in the shoreline and notch on the tree line ahead, taking the channel roughly one-third to the right and two-thirds to the left.

20. **Light 4A and Buoy 5, Battery Islets:** Come nearly abeam of Light 4A to ensure that the ship clears the ledge off the west shore of the Battery Islets. Come to the port with a healthy amount of rudder and steady up on a course of 165 degrees true heading on the point immediately to the west of Lockwood Rock Light 1. Light 4A stands 90 feet outside the channel limit.

    A navigator will notice the ridgeline of Mitkof Island on the port side foreground descending from left to right. In the foreground on the starboard side, the ridgeline of Woewodski Island descends from right to left. The heading of 165 degrees true is nearly where these two ridgelines intersect in a v-notch. For larger vessels, the course from Light 4A to Buoy 2A is frequently a sweeping midchannel swing. Currents can be strong when rounding the Battery Islets. Watch for a set to the west or starboard during either the flood or the ebb.

21. **Buoy 3 and Buoy 2A:** Turn when Buoy 3 is on the starboard bow or when the VRM set to 0.08 NM touches Buoy 3. Another aid in turning takes place when Buoy 2A and Light 2 line up. Begin the turn when they are lined up. Watch the channel past Lockwood Rock open up. Steady up on course 142 degrees true heading on the base of an old logging clearcut along the beach ahead. Watch for any set to the starboard toward Lockwood Rock Light.

22. **Lockwood Rock Light 1:** Turn to the starboard when Lockwood Rock Light 1 is past abeam and December Point Light DP becomes visible from behind the Point Lockwood Light PL and come to a course of 162 degrees true. Steady the ship's heading on the mountain saddle on the side of the Mitkof Island ridgeline ahead and below the top of the mountain. Light 2 is 30 feet outside the channel limit.

23. **Point Lockwood Light PL:** Begin the turn when Point Lockwood Light PL is on the starboard bow or when Deception Point breaks open from behind Point Lockwood. Come to the starboard and steady up on a course of 190 degrees true. Shape up for a distance off Midway Rock Light of 0.15 NM. Vessels frequently anchor up in the bight south of December Point or Deception Point. Some may require a slow down; otherwise, it is allowable to bring the vessel to full speed, conditions permitting.

24. **Midway Rock Light MR:** Come abeam and change course to port steadying up on course 175 degrees true to pass 0.50 NM off of Point Alexander.

    Note: Be aware of the shoal water off Woewodski Island on the west side of the entrance between Point Alexander and Midway Rock.

25. **Point Alexander Light, the exit into eastern Sumner Strait:** If going to Wrangell or Stikine Strait, allow the Point Alexander Light to pass toward the stern to the port quarter. Then change

course to the port and steady up on a course of 104 degrees true. If going to Snow Passage or Sumner Strait, come abeam of the Point Alexander Light and change the course to the starboard to a course of 210 degrees true for Vichnefski Rock.

Bibliography

Betz, Clinton H. "The Alaska Marine Highway, 1948–1989." *The Sea Chest: Journal of the Puget Sound Maritime Historical Society* 26, no. 2 (December 1992).

Bradford, Gershom. *The Mariner's Dictionary.* Barre, MA: Barre Publishers, 1972.

Bushnell, Sharon. "Southeast Mariner, Ellis Lundin." *Anchorage Daily News*, August 22, 2004.

Crenshaw, Russell Sydnor. *Naval Shiphandling.* 4th ed. Annapolis, MD: Naval Institute Press, 1974.

Davidson, George. *Coast Pilot of Alaska: First Part, From Southern Boundary to Cook's Inlet.* Washington: Government Printing Office, 1869.

DeArmond, Robert N. "Sitka Names and Places, Around & About Alaska, Notes and Comments." *Sitka Sentinel*, October 22, 1998.

———. "Peril Strait, Part 3, Around & About Alaska, Notes and Comments." *Sitka Sentinel*, November 11, 1998.

———. "Peril Strait, Part 7, Around & About Alaska, Notes and Comments." *Sitka Sentinel*, December 10, 1998.

———. "Peril Strait, Part 8, Around & About Alaska, Notes and Comments." *Sitka Sentinel*, December 17, 1998.

———. "Peril Strait, Part 9, Around & About Alaska, Notes and Comments." *Sitka Sentinel*, December 24, 1998.

———. "Peril Strait, Part 15, Here and There." *Sitka Sentinel*, February 11, 1999.

———. "Peril Strait, Part 30, Around & About Alaska." *Sitka Sentinel*, May 27, 1999.

———. "Alaska Voyages of USS *Newbern* The Third, Fourth, and Fifth Voyages: Part II, Conclusion." *The Sea Chest, Journal of the Puget Sound Maritime Historical Society* 31 (September 2002).

Farwell, Captain R. F. *Captain Farwell's Hansen Handbook for Piloting in the Inland Waters of The Puget Sound Area, British Columbia, Southeastern Alaska, Southwestern Alaska, Western Alaska.* Seattle: L & H Printing Company, 1951.

Hulley, Clarence C. *Alaska Past and Present.* 3rd ed. Portland, OR: Binford & Mort, 1970.

Janelle, Rick. *Unified Command After Action Report,* M/V *LECONTE Response.* Marine Safety Office, US Coast Guard, Juneau, Alaska, May 21, 2004.

Light List—Pacific Coast and Pacific Islands. Volume VI. Washington, DC: US Government Printing Office, 2011.

M/V *LeConte* Marine Accident Brief, Accident Number DCA-04-MM-020. National Transportation Safety Board, Washington, DC, July 28, 2005.

O'Harra, Doug. "Whale Likely Killed in Collision with Boat." *Anchorage Daily News,* October 21, 2005, p. B1.

Orth, Donald J. *Dictionary of Alaska Place Names.* Washington, DC: US Government Printing Office, 1967.

Pacific Coast Pilot—Alaska, Part 1. Washington: Government Printing Office, 1883.

Pacific Coast Pilot, Part 1: Dixon Entrance to Yakutat Bay with Inland Passage From Strait of Fuca to Dixon Entrance. 3rd ed. Washington: Government Printing Office, 1891.

Pierce, Richard A. *Russian America: A Biographical Dictionary.* Fairbanks: The Limestone Press, 1990.

Pope, Shelly. "AMHS Celebrates 50 years in Southeast." *Petersburg Pilot* XXXIX, no. 18 (May 13, 2013): 4.

Rodgers, Joel W. "Alaska By Ferry." *Alaska Airlines Magazine,* February 1981.

Schmidt, John W. *Ship Handling—Destroyers.* US Naval Admiral, United States Navy, c. 1950.

Smith, Sonya M. Letter to the Editor. *Juneau Empire,* May 16, 2004.

Southeast Alaska Pilot, From Dixon Entrance to Cook Inlet. 6th ed. Hydrographer of the Navy, United Kingdom, 1993.

United States Coast Guard Navigation Rules/International-Inland. US Department of Transportation, 1983.

United States Coast Pilot—Alaska: *Part 1, Dixon Entrance to Yakutat Bay.* 6th ed. Washington: Government Printing Office, 1917.

United States Coast Pilot—Alaska: Part 1, Dixon Entrance to Yakutat Bay. 8th ed. Washington: US Government Printing Office, 1932.

United States Coast Pilot 8, Pacific Coast of Alaska: Dixon Entrance to Cape Spencer. Washington, DC: US Department of Commerce, National Oceanic and Atmospheric Administration (NOAA), 1990.

Unpublished Materials

Carnes, Captain Wayne, Alaska Marine Highway System. Personal unpublished piloting notes on Peril Strait and Sergius Narrows, Juneau, Alaska, December 15, 2006.

Dagle, Captain Tillman, Alaska Marine Highway System. Personal unpublished piloting notes for Peril Strait, Neva and Olga Straits, c. 1970.

DeArmond, Robert. Personal letter on the USCG *Clover,* Sitka, Alaska, August 24, 2007.

Johnson, Captain Robert M., Alaska Marine Highway System. Personal unpublished piloting notes on Olga Strait, c. 1990.

M/V *Aurora,* official logbook pages, February 10–19, 1982, Archive Box J19445, Records & Information Management Program, Lemon Creek Warehouse, Alaska State Archives, Juneau.

Roppel, Patricia. Unpublished and undated history notes on Peril Strait, Neva and Olga Straits, Wrangell, Alaska, c. 1990.

Acknowledgments

Wrangell Narrows

I wish to thank Mr. Stephen Kinney of Ketchikan, whose suggestion led to this book. I also thank Captain Erv Hagerup, Captain Scott Macaulay, Captain Charles Bates, Captain Phil Taylor, Captain Fred Montez, Captain James Doran, Captain Harvey Williamson, Captain Wayne Carnes, Captain Alan Doty, Captain Jeff Baken, and many others who have shared information and reviewed this document to try to achieve an accurate representation of Wrangell Narrows. I am very grateful to all who have taught me about Wrangell Narrows, whether by direct instruction or observed actions.

I am forever indebted to several senior masters in particular: Captain Richard Twain Hofstad, Captain Harold Payne, and Captain Maynard Reeser. I also wish to mention two chief mates who helped me when I first started my career with the Alaska Marine Highway System. They are Mr. Kenneth Mayo and Mr. Thomas Scott. These mariners were wonderful mentors, sharing their expertise on piloting the wasters of Alaska. To all, named and unnamed, I remain very grateful.

Lastly, I reserve special thanks to my original self-publisher of Wrangell Narrows, Scott Graber, Scott Company Publishing, and to Steve Kinney and Captain Dale Miller of the Marine Transportation Department, University of Alaska Southeast, Ketchikan, for their encouragement and faith in this work.

Peril Strait

I am grateful to the many fine officers and captains of the Alaska Marine Highway System who have taught piloting Peril Strait with patience and example over many years. I am equally grateful to the ship pilots of the Southeast Alaska Pilots Association for sharing their in-depth knowledge of Sitka Sound.

There are many who have shared information about Peril Strait with me over the years, but those listed below are truly noteworthy:

- The late Alaskan historian and journalist Robert DeArmond of Sitka allowed me to study and use his many articles on Peril Strait. An impeccable source for historical detail, he was a man who loved Southeastern Alaska.
- Alaskan historian Patricia Roppel allowed me to study and use her unpublished notes on Peril Strait, including Olga and Neva Straits. These notes reveal gems of information not found anywhere else.
- Captain Wayne Carnes of the Alaska Marine Highway System's FVF *Fairweather* shared knowledge and photographs of Sergius Narrows during maximum current. Seeing Sergius Narrows at maximum current is something few of us have the opportunity to witness.
- Captain Matthew Wilkens of the Alaska Marine Highway System, a man skilled with his camera, shared several of his photographs of Peril Strait.
- Retired Alaska Marine Highway System Bos'n Ellis Lundin of Ketchikan showed me his prized piece of West Francis Rock that rests in his yard and imparted his recollections of the 1974 grounding of the M/V *Columbia* on that rock.
- Able seaman Brian Chinell of Sitka shared his tragic story of the 1986 sinking of the tugboat *Roughneck* in Sergius Narrows.

Many thanks to Danelle Landis for providing words of support and ready answers to questions concerning mechanics and style.

I wish to express my gratitude to Captain Dale Miller of the Marine Department, University of Alaska Southeast Ketchikan, for his encouragement to bring this manuscript into publication. A special thank you to everyone at the University of Alaska Press, including Elizabeth Laska, Laura Walker, Nate Bauer, and Krista West, for their encouragement and assistance, and to the University of Alaska Press advisory board members. A special note of gratitude goes to Ron Kotrc of Ketchikan, whose knowledge of publishing, editing, and formatting made it possible.

Special appreciation goes to Captain Jeff Baken, Southeastern Alaska Pilots Association; Neil Nickerson, UAS Associate Professor of Marine Transportation; and Captain Dale Miller, UAS Ketchikan Campus Marine Transportation Department Head for peer reviewing this document for the University of Alaska Press.

To my wife, Wynn, thank you for your encouragement and editing skills. She dedicated countless hours to this effort. Without her spirited help, this project would have been difficult to bring to light.

Index

Note: page numbers followed by *f*, *t*, and *m* refer to figures, tables, and maps respectively.

D

N

O

Q

R

S

Y